RADICAL TORIES

Other books by Charles Taylor:

Reporter in Red China

Snow Job: Canada, the United States and
Vietnam (1954 to 1973)

Six Journeys: A Canadian Pattern

Charles Taylor

RADICAL TORIES

The Conservative
Tradition in Canada

AFTERWORD BY
RUDYARD GRIFFITHS

ANANSI

Published in 1982 by House of Anansi Press Ltd.

This edition published in 2006 by
House of Anansi Press Inc.
110 Spadina Avenue, Suite 801
Toronto, ON, M5V 2K4
Tel. 416-363-4343
Fax 416-363-1017
www.anansi.ca

Distributed in Canada by
HarperCollins Canada Ltd.
1995 Markham Road
Scarborough, ON, M1B 5M8
Toll free tel. 1-800-387-0117

House of Anansi Press is committed to protecting our natural environment. As part of our efforts, this book is printed on Rolland Enviro paper: it contains 100% post-consumer recycled fibres, is acid-free, and is processed chlorine-free.

10 09 08 07 06   1 2 3 4 5

LIBRARY AND ARCHIVES CANADA CATALOGUING IN PUBLICATION DATA

Taylor, Charles, 1935–
Radical Tories : the conservative tradition in Canada / Charles Taylor ; afterword by Rudyard Griffiths.

Includes bibliographical references and index.
ISBN-13: 978-0-88784-754-7
ISBN-10: 0-88784-754-4

1. Conservatism – Canada – History – 20th century. 2. Progressive Conservative Party of Canada – History – 20th century. 3. Canada – Politics and government – 20th century. I. Title.

JA84.C3T39 2006   320.520971   C2006-902447-2

Library of Congress Control Number: 2006927553

Cover design: Paul Hodgson

Cover illustration: Charles Pachter
The Painted Flag, 1988; acrylic on canvas
Collection: Canadian Embassy, Washington

We acknowledge for their financial support of our publishing program the Canada Council for the Arts, the Ontario Arts Council, and the Government of Canada through the Book Publishing Industry Development Program (BPIDP).

Canada Council   Conseil des Arts
for the Arts   du Canada

ONTARIO ARTS COUNCIL
CONSEIL DES ARTS DE L'ONTARIO

Printed and bound in Canada

Contents

To Scott Symons

Preface

This is the story of a journey into the Canadian conservative tradition. When I set out on that journey in the summer of 1978, I was far from certain where it would lead me. Like many Canadians, however, I was baffled by the pettiness and anger which wracked our public life. Amid our constitutional squabbles and regional jealousies—as well as our apparently insoluble economic dilemmas—we all seemed peevish and despairing. While much of this could be blamed on the divisive tactics of our political leaders, I sensed that our malaise had deeper roots. For several decades, Canadians had lived with the rhetoric of a dominant liberal ideology which placed few limits on man's freedom to shape his future, and which envisaged unprecedented technological achievement and material abundance. Clearly this dream had gone awry, and I began to suspect that liberalism was incapable of answering our aspirations. At the same time, I was aware that more and more Canadians, searching for an alternative, were turning to conservative thinkers such as George Grant who spoke to us from the heart of an older and very different tradition. It was that tradition which I set out to explore, even though I had doubts about its relevance.

By the time I ended my inquiries in the spring of 1982, I was more than a little surprised at my conclusions. Initially pessimistic, I have grown much more sanguine. For I found a conservative heritage which is far from moribund, and which relates directly to our present needs. It is also very much our own tradition, for it is neither mired in nostalgic anglophilia, nor obsessed with the contemporary American fad of neo-conservatism. Populist and even radical, it has a particular Canadian tang.   .

This book could not have been written without the assistance of its protagonists. I am especially grateful to the late Donald G. Creighton, the late William L. Morton, Al Purdy, Eugene Forsey, George Grant, Robert Stanfield and David Crombie.

Both William Kilbourn and Tom Symons were extremely helpful. When the text was starting to take shape, Sean Kane made several incisive suggestions.

This is the third of my books which has had James Polk as its editor. For such a creative collaboration, I give deep and lasting thanks.

I should also like to thank others who gave important assistance: James Bacque, Jay Cody, Luella Creighton, Dr. Ralph L. Curry, Ramsay Derry, Roy Faibish, Doug Fetherling, Shirley Gibson, Sheila Grant, Aaron Klokeid, Dennis Lee, F. W. O. Morton, Mrs. W. L. Morton, Stephen Patrick, Barney Sandwell, Denis Smith, Fred Taylor, Vincent Tovell and David Williams.

For more than 35 years, Scott Symons has been my closest friend. Apart from his many insights and criticisms, this book has gained from his exhortations. The dedication honours not only such specific contributions, but also those decades of mirthful and tumultuous camaraderie.

I

A Special Destiny:
Leacock, Sandwell and Deacon

In these grudging and perplexed times, it is hard to credit the enthusiasm with which Canadians once regarded their country and its future. There is much distemper in the land; we seem to have become baffled and parochial. Yet during the first quarter of this century, Canadians developed a heady self-confidence which was based on practical achievement and an almost unbridled optimism. As Donald Creighton wrote: "During those twenty-five creative and expansive years, Canada had settled a half-continent, fought a great war, changed an empire into a commonwealth, and helped, in a small way, to found the world's first international organization. It was a long and crowded record of accomplishment, and it got under way so swiftly and with such explosive force at the beginning of the century that the pace of progress seemed likely to continue undiminished until its end. When Stephen Leacock confidently predicted that Canada would have a population of a hundred million by the year 2000, he was being soberly realistic and not intentionally funny."

Leacock made his prediction in 1907. It was part of a pamphlet, *Greater Canada: An Appeal*, which is one of the most eloquent of all arguments for a special Canadian destiny. Its author is important, not only as the world-famous humourist (in 1907, that was still in the future), but also as one of the most influential of Canadian nationalists. A Victorian who lived to see World War Two, Leacock provides a link between the statesmen who created Canada and later generations of conservative patriots. His vision of Canada has long been overtaken by events, and much of it may strike us as merely quaint. But none of it is narrow or provincial; rather, it resounds with that pride and vigor which, as Creighton noted, set the tone for decades yet to come—and which we now have largely lost.

Leacock liked to mention that the year of his birth—1869—was the exact middle of Queen Victoria's reign. During his boyhood, Victoria's empire reached its pinnacle of size and power, and there seemed no reason to doubt that all those red patches on the map (an expanding Canada was by far the largest) would last forever. It was a confident, expansive age in which the enthusiasts of empire preached a doctrine which stressed the self-evident superiority of the white man and his moral obligations to the so-called lesser breeds. In 1887, Joseph Chamberlain, then a rising young British politician, lectured a Toronto audience about "the greatness and importance of the destiny which is reserved for the Anglo-Saxon race ... infallibly predestined to be the predominating force in the future history and civilization of the world."

There is no record that Leacock—who was then preparing to enter the University of Toronto on a modest scholarship—attended the lecture. Within two years, however, he would be teaching at Upper Canada College where he came under the powerful influence of the headmaster, Sir George Parkin, who was among the leaders of the Canadian Imperialists. Energetic, lucid, and filled with passionate conviction, Parkin called himself "a wandering evangelist of Empire" — before coming to UCC he had travelled to many of its outposts and published three books advocating imperial unity. This cause was at the heart of contemporary political debate, since few articulate Canadians were satisfied with the existing colonial relationship. There were those, like Goldwin Smith, who held that Canada's destiny lay in continental union with the United States. At the other extreme, the Imperialists argued that Canada should be much more assertive in seeking influence — and even leadership — within the Empire.

Along with a fellow teacher, William L. Grant, Leacock became an eager disciple of the Imperialist cause. But there was a significant difference of emphasis between the two generations. Fearing annexation by the United States, Parkin and his contemporaries had been concerned to preserve the British connection without unduly questioning Ottawa's subservience to London. By the turn of the century, with settlers flooding the prairies and the nation apparently launched on a period of unprecedented growth, the younger imperialists were espousing their cause with greater self-confidence and a burgeoning conviction that Canada was destined to achieve equality with Britain inside the Empire, and possibly even to surpass her. Staunch nationalists, they also rejected extreme forms of anglophilia. According to Carl Berger, both Grant and Leacock thought that Parkin placed too much stress on refined manners and an English accent, and that he mentioned his English acquaintances too often. "Has he no friends below the rank of Viscount?" Grant asked Leacock. "Plenty," Leacock replied, "—back on the farm."

Leacock was soon to succeed Parkin as the Empire's itinerant evangelist. After post-graduate work at the University of Chicago, he went on staff at McGill in 1901. Five years later he published *Elements of Political Science*. Straightforward and scholarly, this basic text was an immediate success. Translated into eighteen languages, it was to remain Leacock's best-selling book; it also established his academic reputation. But it was the much shorter essay, *Greater Canada: An Appeal*, which confirmed Leacock as one of the most eloquent of the Imperialists. At the request of the Governor-General, Lord Grey, Leacock had been lecturing on the Empire to enthusiastic audiences throughout eastern Canada; in his essay he preached the cause with equal fervor.

Proclaiming "the inevitable greatness of Canada," Leacock writes lyrically of its enormous size and vast resources. All it lacks is people, but its population is "growing, growing, growing, with a march that will make us ten millions tomorrow, twenty millions in our children's time and a hundred millions ere yet the century runs out." He rejects both independence ("Independent we could not survive a decade") and union with the United States ("They have chosen their lot; we have chosen ours"). Instead, Canada can best fulfil its destiny as an equal partner in the Empire. Leacock acknowledges that imperialism is a tainted word for many Canadians: "It is too much associated with a truckling subservience to English people and English ideas and the silly swagger of the hop-o'my-thumb junior officer." But he is advocating a higher imperialism: " . . . the imperialism of the plain man at the plough and the clerk in the counting house, the imperialism of any decent citizen that demands for this country its proper place in the councils of the Empire and in the destiny of the world. In this sense, imperialism means but the realization of a Greater Canada, the recognition of a wider citizenship." Although he is hazy on the details, Leacock seems to favour an imperial council and an imperial parliament in which Canada would have significant representation. Addressing his words to the polit-

icians assembling in London for the fourth Colonial Conference, he says that the Canadians should tell the British: "We
will be your colony no longer. Make us one with you in an
Empire, Permanent and Indivisible."

Now it was time for the Governor-General to advocate
"turning Dr. Leacock loose . . . as an Imperial missionary."
With the backing of McGill and the Cecil Rhodes Trust, the
37-year-old professor and his wife sailed from Halifax in the
spring of 1907. Following the path Parkin had blazed twenty
years earlier, Leacock was on tour for a year, lecturing to
large and admiring audiences in England, Australia, New
Zealand, South Africa and the Canadian west. Despite this
triumphant progress, there were signs that the Canadian
might be a bit too prickly in his nationalism to be an ideal
replacement for Parkin. Even Lord Grey had criticised his
earlier Canadian lectures as too anti-American. ("It is quite
possible to crow and flap one's wings without treading on
one's neighbour's corns.") In London, Leacock caused considerable offense when he wrote a newspaper article which
deplored the lack of progress towards imperial unity and
described John Bull as an aging farmer too set in his ways:
"The old man's got old and he don't know it; can't kick him
off the place; but I reckon that the next time we come
together to talk things over the boys have got to step right in
and manage the whole farm." The British were hardly
accustomed to such pungent advice from the colonies;
Winston Churchill called it "offensive twaddle."

In 1911, when the Liberal government of Sir Wilfred
Laurier advocated reciprocity with the United States — and
called a general election on the issue — Leacock sprang to the
support of the Conservatives. Newspapers across Canada
carried full-page advertisements, written by Leacock, which
argued that the Liberals were selling out the nation. In both
Ontario and Quebec, he campaigned vigorously for Conservative candidates. Eugene Forsey, later a colleague of
Leacock's at McGill, recalled that his trump card was a copy

of a letter from President Taft to ex-President Roosevelt. "He'd build up a great dramatic presentation. 'Do you know what I have here?' he'd ask, pulling out the letter from his breast pocket and reading it with a flourish of indignation. He made great play of Taft's assertion that reciprocity would make Canada an 'adjunct' of the United States. He always said that a short word with a lot of consonants—like 'adjunct'—was one to emphasize and pound the table at. In fact, he knew the letter off by heart and often pulled out his laundry list or the hotel dinner menu." In the end, the Conservatives won a decisive victory, and Leacock was given much of the credit for the defeat of a Liberal cabinet minister in his native Orillia. In Leacock's view, the election had been "a plebescite of eight million people on this half of the continent in expression of their wish for an enduring union with the Empire."

This was Leacock's final fling as an imperial missionary. When a new edition of *Elements of Political Science* appeared in 1921, he no longer presented imperial federation as a practical possibility, conceding that "the events of the war have entirely changed the outlook. All proposals for a formal federation and for a supreme parliament and for pan-imperial taxes are drifting into the background of academic discussion." This was simple realism. As Creighton later noted, World War One was a watershed in Canada's external relations. Apart from the fact that an exhausted Britain had no heart for dreams of imperial grandeur, Canada's own interests were increasingly directed to the south. After the war, Canadian exports to the United States began to rival the value of exports to Britain, and the old transcontinental, transatlantic trading axis ceased to be the main line of Canadian commercial endeavour. Then the nineteen-twenties saw the advent of Mackenzie King, doggedly fighting the paper tiger of British colonialism while leading Canada on the path of ever closer ties to the United States. Leacock always hated King for this: if he had to acknowledge the impossibility of imperial federation, his faith in the Anglo-Canadian connection never wavered. As a younger colleague at McGill described Leacock's lectures in the nineteen-thirties: "He, before Winston Churchill, saved the British Empire every Monday, Wednesday and Friday at 3 o'clock in room 20."

Reading Leacock — and reading about him — I came to accept that his crusty defence of the Empire was an expression of Canadian patriotism which was quite legitimate in its day, if since overtaken by events. But my understanding came from books: despite the marvellous body of Leacockian anecdotes, I lacked a direct appreciation of how he lived his loyalties. And so, on a hunch, I chose a warm summer day to drive up to Orillia. By his choice of homes, a man tells a lot about himself. If Leacock was long gone, I might at least evoke his shade on the shores of Old Brewery Bay.

First impressions were hardly promising. To reach Leacock's house, you turn off the main road opposite a glut of fast food shops — a Kentucky Fried Chicken, a Big Burger and a Pop Shoppe. Next you pass under a shoddy, wooden, mock-triumphal arch. At the end of the driveway, the first thing you encounter is an ancient bus, tarted up with flower boxes and proclaiming itself The Old Brewery Bay Gift Shop. It sells T-shirts, plastic purses, mugs, postcards and similar tourist bait. The chronicler of bustling Mariposa (a thinly disguised Orillia) might well be offended by the present scene, but he would hardly be surprised. You can almost hear the famous chuckle.

And I *do* hear it . . . that's the eerie part . . . coming from the garden. Only it turns out to be an actor, dressed in a typical Leacock suit (well-cut, shabby and unpressed), recreating Leacock the public story-teller for a camera and a score of film technicians. They've completely taken over the place . . . with their cables, lights and generators they're like an occupation army. Even the tourists have been banished as the film makers complete a pilot program which they hope will launch a lucrative television series. It may be good, of course, and faithful to its subject, but it seems another rip-off. People cashing in.

But the home . . . the home redeems everything. It's a rambling, two-storied house with a lot of white stucco and graceful porches and balconies. Mainly it's an old Ontario summer home in the grand Edwardian manner, but there is something more . . . an echo of an English country manor (a squire's house) *and* a French feeling to the exterior, something in the pitch of the high roof which suggests a seignieury from Normandy or Quebec. Inside, the fireplaces, the wicker furniture and the dark oak panelling add a further touch of simple elegance and substance.

The house was designed by an architect, but to Leacock's careful sketches and specifications. Instinctively he created a home which reflected what he had become: the Ontario farm boy who made good, the yeoman squire with the inclinations of an English gent and a touch of gallic flair. His Ontario roots, and the English and French strains which were part of his Canadian heritage: all are present in that eloquent home. As much as any book which I had read, it was a good starting point for my journey into conservative tradition.

It was some time before that tradition lost its sense of pride and optimism. Despite the death of the imperial dream after World War One, despite King's uninspiring leadership, there was no immediate weakening of the confidence with which leading Canadians regarded their nation's future. If their visions were often less anglophile and more continentalist than Leacock's, they still pulsed with grandeur. Among the enthusiasts was B. K. Sandwell, the editor of *Saturday Night* for two decades and one of Canada's most influential men-of-letters. In 1930, Sandwell published a small book called *Our Canada* which was a stirring paean to the nation:

" . . . a land where nature puts strength and purpose into the souls of men and builds a breed that rises indominitable before vicissitudes, and forges ever ahead with the calmness of courage and the certainty of a great destiny that must not be denied . . . . . Canada! The land with the courage to be great!"

An even more remarkable effusion was published in 1933. This was *My Vision of Canada* by William Arthur Deacon, another influential essayist who was the long-time book reviewer for both *The Mail and Empire* and its successor, *The Globe and Mail*. With unchecked enthusiasm, Deacon told his fellow Canadians to prepare themselves for world leadership: "I believe that before the year 2000 Canada's world dominance will be as undisputed a fact as any commonplace of history." Despite the onset of the Depression, Deacon argued that Canada's future greatness was assured by its vast natural resources, by the prospect of industrialization and increased trade, and by the bold leadership that would emerge through the blending of different European strains. Canada, he proclaimed, would be the home of "the new racial type, the neo-European, with the strength of the Teuton, the nimble wit of the French and the Celts; and the mixture tuned up to the necessary pitch of nervous tension, capable of catching a New World vision, by the smaller yet potent strains of romance and spiritual discernment to be gained from the minority elements, once unfortunately despised."

Almost in passing, Deacon scornfully dismissed any threat to Canada from the United States, whether through annexation or economic domination, and was certain that English and French Canadians would soon overcome the artificial divisions of language and religion. He cautioned only that Canada should avoid ever again becoming entangled in a European conflict. For its own self-defence, the nation had no need of a large army and massive armaments. Since the next war would be fought from the sky, Canada could rely on its commercial aircraft, each of which could be adapted into fighting craft in one hour, by mounting guns or providing carrying apparatus for bombs. These would be sufficient in "the very unlikely contingency of a sudden attempt at invasion. If such a situation arose, the act of converting planes would be similar to that of the farmers in 1812, who reached down the guns they kept for bears and deer, and went off to guard the frontier."

Left in peace, Canada would surge on to fulfil its destiny. "By the year 2000 it will be apparent enough how truly the 20th century will have been Canada's. By universal acknowledgment, world dominance will have been attained in commerce and in culture. She will exercise undisputed intellectual leadership. Her fundamental strength will lie in the prestige she has won. Rich and powerful herself, with a standard of living unique in history, she will have the undiluted respect of the world, not only for the excellence of her own institutions, but also for the example of intelligent justice in both internal and external dealings. This will be the characteristic by which her golden age will be remembered, as Rome is acclaimed for her organizing ability." Because Canada would be building on sound foundations, Deacon concluded, her golden age would last for five centuries.

After only fifty years, it is easy to laugh at such effusions. It might be better to weep. This is no time for visions. Of course, it is easy to be skeptical about that earlier optimistic rhetoric—even at the time it must have sounded windy. But I suspected there was something to it, something genuine which had given courage and faith to earlier generations of Canadians. I wanted to discover what it was, and whether it was lost for good.

I start with Leacock because he was a fervent exponent of the conservative nationalism which derived from Sir John A. Macdonald and which proclaimed Canada's destiny with so much confidence. Clearly there is much in Leacock's toryism which is now outdated, but it still seems infinitely more attractive than the mean and grudging doctrine which came to the fore after World War One and which has since largely dominated our conceptions of Canada and its place in the world. This new liberal version of Canadian history had Mackenzie King as its spiritual godfather, and a host of academics, journalists and civil servants as its prime mythologists. It is, of course, that stirring chronicle which charts our progress from colony to nation, from the shackles of British rule to the lucrative alliance with our friendly neighbors to the south. In partisan terms, this approach could be used to portray the Grits as both patriotic and progressive, and the Conservatives as reactionary anglophiles. It was all very plausible and liberal ... it was, in fact, a variant of the Whig Interpretation of History: a tendency, in Herbert Butterfield's words, " ... to emphasize certain principles of progress in the past and to produce a story which is the ratification if not the glorification of the present." It was also very convenient, especially to those like King and his foreign affairs mentor, O. D. Skelton. Both were obsessive in asserting Canada's independence of Britain. Both were generally oblivious to the threat of American domination. If the desired conclusions were not supported by some of the facts—Britain had not seriously hindered the growth of Canadian nationhood; the United States had posed the only real threat to Canadian territorial and political integrity—those recalcitrant details would be suppressed. Nothing could be allowed to impinge upon the new Authorized Version; nothing could be allowed to impede the Liberals from fulfilling their role as our natural governing party.

All that may suggest, on my part, a certain bias. If so, it should be qualified. While I yield to no man in my suspicion of the Grits, I have seldom been much of a partisan. When growing up, I could never support the Conservatives—in their different ways, both Drew and Diefenbaker appalled me. Since then, I had been persuaded only rarely that the party had the slightest idea of what it was about. Nor was I ready to blame all our misfortunes on King and his successors, despite their malign domination of our federal politics. My concern went deeper than party rivalries, although it did implicate the Liberals. Much more than Canadian conservatives and Canadian socialists, the Grits embodied the forces of that liberal ideology which George Grant has described as the dominant influence of the modern era, and which pulls us all toward a universal and homogeneous state of almost certain tyranny. I sensed it was this ideology which had sapped out pride and eroded our particularity. If there was an alternative (on this point, I was far from certain), perhaps it was a derivation of the earlier tory tradition, with all its spunk and vigor.

And so I set out upon my journey into that tradition. From the start I recognized my limitations: the West was largely foreign to me, and I had no qualifications to write about Quebec. This latter was a particular handicap, since I knew that French Canadians had their own conservative tradition with many important parallels to that of English Canada. But I lacked the language, and hence full access to that major part of my heritage. Still, there was much to explore on the English-speaking side, and I had some idea of where to look, and whom to approach. Again, I was not concerned with partisan politics: instead I would concentrate on writers and artists who had a tory touch and who might guide me on my way. Inevitably (it now seems) I began with the grandest old conservative of them all.

II
The Northern Empire:
Donald Creighton

During his last two decades, Donald Creighton lived with
his wife Luella in a red brick farmhouse in the village of
Brooklin, about thirty miles east of Toronto along the old
Highway Seven. In anticipation of his retirement from the
University of Toronto, Canada's foremost historian had
sought his roots on a nineteenth century street in the
heartland of rural Ontario. It is a short street with other
red-and-white brick homes and a towering Methodist church
at the end: a mid-Victorian street of lilac bushes and tidy
gardens suggesting yeoman squires, comfortable families,
simple pleasures and unchallenged verities. If Princess
Street seems prim and puritanical today, there is also a touch
of elegance—restrained elegance—to those stolid dwellings.
Neither rustic nor city-slick, it is a street where gentlefolk
have always lived, where manners have always counted, and
where peace and order still prevail.

I drove to Brooklin on three occasions during Creighton's last year. (He died in his sleep on the night of December 18, 1979, at the age of 77.) He had agreed to help me with this book, he had spoken and written generous things about its predecessors, and he had scorned my disavowal of the proper academic qualifications. As he put it in a letter: "I feel confident that you are far better fitted to undertake the study you propose than any of the current crop of young professional historians, most of whom seem quite incapable of writing a work of analysis and interpretation, or indeed, a major work of any kind." That was my first experience of Creighton's legendary acerbity: there would be many more.

On my first two visits, Creighton met me in the living room, leaning heavily on a cane. (Later he would be confined to a wheel chair.) Always tall and angular, he was now stooped, haggard and very frail. But he was cleanly shaven and impeccably dressed in a blue-grey suit with a shirt and tie in other shades of blue, and his manner was courtly. (I was not just greeted; I was *received.*) For Creighton to sit down was a lengthy exercise, full of pain and labour, but once settled in his chair, he would look up with a beaming, winsome smile, (quite precisely, it lit up his face), and the old, collapsing body became almost invisible, subdued and dominated by the high-domed, oracular head. And then the voice would boom out—deep and orotund, the phrases almost as rich and rhythmical as any in his books—the voice of a Victorian Methodist preacher (such as his father had been) launched on a tumult of castigation and exhortation.

Not that he ignored his illness: apart from the discomfort, his exasperation was palpable. "Old men wear out!" he roared, adding that although his mind was still sharp ("I'm all right up here, thank God!"), he could no longer use his hand to write and had never been comfortable with a dictating machine. ("I need to see the words on the page.") As his final work, he had hoped to write a memoir of his mother, but now he realised this would never happen. There was a long pause. "I think I should die," he finally said. "What's the point in hanging on?" Then he mentioned that he had tried to get pills from one of his doctors, so that he could end himself. (For once this came out quietly, almost under his breath.) Suddenly his eyes sparkled and danced, as he described one of the nurses who had been attending him. After a eulogy of her physical presence, he stopped abruptly, as if recollecting himself, and sadly said: "Oh, my . . ."

Yet these were mere preliminaries. For soon (and this was true of each visit), Creighton would be launched on his big subject—almost his only subject—his beloved Canada. Then it would all come out—his rooted faith in Sir John A. Macdonald's original vision, in British traditions and in strong central government, as well as his total disdain for all Liberals and Americans, collaborators in our downfall, in our loss of independence. "Well, it's still a good place to live, but that's all Canada is now—just a good place to live." This, too, was said quietly, but most of the rest was roared, as if he were addressing not a single guest but an audience of thousands, of many generations, on the subject of our self-betrayal. His vehemence was implacable. My second visit, in the spring of 1979, came just after the Conservatives had won a federal election, but had been denied an overall majority by the voters of Quebec. "The French Canadians always vote Liberal," Creighton bellowed. "It's not something they think about. It's a bodily function—like urinating and defecating!" In his books, Creighton castigates Mackenzie King above all other Liberals; now he claimed that Lester Pearson was even worse—"I feel positive hatred toward that man"—and indicated that Pierre Trudeau was almost beneath his contempt. As for Americans—"I have an incredible dislike and hatred of the United States. I've always had it. I never met one I liked." Nor did the emerging nations emerge unscathed: "All those ranks of grinning, idiot black faces at the United

Nations . . . " He paused. "I guess I'm what they call a racist."
Somehow he sounded both abashed and unrepentant.

By now I was feeling distinctly uneasy. These were surely
the rantings of a dying man: they could be excused but should
never be reported. Yet Creighton was far from senility, and
I knew that even in his prime, he had never masked his
prejudices. A friend had told me how he once sat behind
Creighton at a public lecture given by his fellow historian
Arthur Lower. To Creighton, the eminent Lower was anathema, mainly because of his liberal bias against the British
tradition as a legitimate part of the Canadian heritage. As
my friend recalled: "Donald kept shouting 'Brain damage...
the man must have brain damage!' He may have thought he
was muttering, but his voice carried all around the hall."
When I told the anecdote to Creighton, he shook with
laughter. Months later, on my final visit, I felt I knew him
well enough to broach the subject of his vehemence, and how
it should be handled. "Perhaps I've been too outspoken," he
conceded, "but you mustn't make me bland. I'm apt to be
more vehement verbally than mentally. I love words. I get
carried away by them. But I *do* have strong, strong feelings.
Everything that hurts the things I love I react against
violently—violently!"

Much as I admired his passion, this failed to settle my
unease. I recalled Leacock's many jibes—much more offensive than amusing—against Germans, blacks and Orientals
—and I wondered whether intolerance, let alone racism, was
a distinctive tory trait. It was not a pleasing speculation. But
I was only at the start of my journey: there would be time to
sort this out.

With Creighton there were moments when the fury
would subside, and something more personal would emerge.
On that earlier trip, I had been asked to stay for tea—no
mere cup and cookie in the living room but a proper English
high tea in the dining room with heaps of chive sandwiches
and a rich fruit cake. As we sat before the massive sideboard
with its photographs of grandparents, under a painting of a

great-grandmother, Creighton was strangely quiet and subdued. We had been talking of literature and especially of the
Victorian and Edwardian novelists whom he had read from
an early age and who had done much to shape his style.
Creighton had been sad and discontented, doubting the
value of his books and asserting that he would have much
preferred to be a novelist, that it was novelists rather than
historians who best probed the mysteries of human behaviour. Then he shunted to his feet and shuffled from the
room. Long minutes later he returned with a book, *The Old
Wives' Tale* by Arnold Bennett. As he fumbled to find a
passage near the end, he said he could never read it without
weeping. Finally he found it, started to read, faltered, shook
his head and passed the book across the table with a sense of
great urgency, as if everything that day had led us to this
point, almost as though it were his final message to me. It is
the passage in which the aging Sophia Scales, filled with a
sense that her life had been barren and useless, is suddenly
confronted with the body of her wastrel husband, 35 years
after he had deserted her:

> Sophia then experienced a pure and primitive
> emotion, uncoloured by any moral or religious
> quality. She was not sorry that Gerald had wasted
> his life, nor that he was a shame to his years and to
> her. The manner of his life was of no importance.
> What affected her was that he had once been
> young, and that he had grown old, and was now
> dead. That was all. Youth and vigor had come to
> that. He had ill-treated her; he had abandoned
> her; he had been a devious rascal; but how trivial
> were such accusations against him! The whole of
> her huge and bitter grievance against him fell to
> pieces and crumbled. She saw him young, and
> proud, and strong, as for instance when he had
> kissed her lying on the bed in that London hotel —
> she forgot the name — in 1866; and now he was old,

and worn, and horrible, and dead. It was the riddle of life that was puzzling and killing her. By the corner of her eye, reflected in a wardrobe near the bed, she glimpsed a tall, forlorn woman, who had once been young and now was old. He and she had once loved and burned and quarrelled in the glittering and scornful pride of youth. But time had worn them out. 'Yet a little while,' she thought, 'and I shall be lying on a bed like that! And what shall I have lived for? What is the meaning of it?' The riddle of life was killing her, and she seemed to drown in a sea of inexpressible sorrow.

As I handed the book back, Creighton said nothing. But his whole body was trembling, his hands were clutching hard at the table, his eyes were enormous, and his look was terrible, commanding and beseeching me to understand.

Little more was said that day. As I took my leave, Creighton stood in the doorway, gaunt and frail and splendidly doughty. "In the name of God!" he shouted, "come back *soon!*"

I did make one more trip to Brooklin—as it turned out, only two weeks before Creighton's death. Again we talked of politics and literature. Again what struck me hardest was Creighton's repeated assertion that Canada had failed to achieve its destiny, and was now nothing more than "a good place to live." This time, however, his pessimism was a shade less implacable. "We're not quite doomed ... not yet," he told me. "But for the life of me, I can't see what there's *left* to bring us back together."

We were sitting in his study, a simple and austere room which Creighton had added to the original farmhouse. On every wall, the shelves were crammed with books, including

Creighton's many volumes. In these, in soaring prose, he had given us his own vision of that Canadian destiny, and a trenchant account of its betrayal. For years the books had awed me with their power, and convinced me with their lucidity. In recent months I had come to love their author for his zest and passion, his courage and courtliness, his sheer panache. Yet I felt myself resisting Creighton's pessimism—partly because it seemed to contradict that spirit; partly because I had a stubborn instinct that not everything was lost. But Creighton had posed a formidable challenge at the start of my journey. Before going any farther, I had to come to terms with both the vision and the visionary.

Literature was his earliest passion. Creighton grew up in Toronto before and during World War One, in a house that was filled with books. Almost every evening, his mother would read to him at length: "...the Bible, Tennyson and especially huge dollops of Dickens. I was steeped in great writing." His father, William B. Creighton, was a Methodist minister who edited *The Christian Guardian*. A man of liberal tastes and progressive outlook, the elder Creighton was assiduous in reviewing all the latest novels and poetry. "He used to come home on the street car with great packages of books under his arm," his son recalled. "I claimed the right to open the packages. I was always beside myself with excitement." He was also allowed to read the books, and eventually to try his hand at reviewing some of them. Soon he was at home with all the great novelists of the late nineteenth and early twentieth centuries, among them Dickens, Thackeray, Trollope, Hardy, Bennett and Galsworthy, as well as Balzac, Zola and even Proust. They became a lasting legacy.

Creighton entered Victoria College in the University of Toronto in 1921, to take an honours degree in History and English. For him, the two disciplines would always be linked. On the side of literature, professors such as E. J. Pratt and Pelham Edgar reinforced his early enthusiasm, but Creighton came increasingly under the sway of a group of younger historians, especially J. B. Brebner, George Smith and Hume Wrong. "They were all good lecturers, and they conceived of history as drama—I think that's what converted me to their cause." This zest for the dramatic prompted Creighton to concentrate on the Napoleonic period ("It's full of glorious events") when a scholarship took him to Balliol in Oxford. Returning to Toronto in 1927, he rejoined his old department as an instructor, specializing in European history, notably the French Revolution. At that point he had no interest in Canadian history, but harsh circumstances forced him to change his mind. Newly married, and living on a salary of $1,800, he travelled with Luella to Paris in the summer of 1928 for further study in his chosen field. In those days there were few grants for travel and research, and the Creightons paid their own way. After they ran out of money ("We weren't eating properly at all"), and were forced to return home in steerage, Creighton reluctantly decided he would have to find a specialty that was more within his means. "It was a terrible moment," he recalled. "I desperately wanted to write something, but I knew I had to give up European history. So I decided to find a Canadian subject. It was a poor second. I had a real sense of deprivation."

On the advice of an older colleague, Creighton spent the summer of 1930 in Ottawa, working in the Public Archives on the papers of Lord Dalhousie, governor-in-chief of Canada in the eighteen-twenties. The idea was to use the recently acquired papers as the basis of a small book which might also earn a Ph.D. But Creighton found it hard slogging. Ottawa was not the liveliest of places ("After Paris, I hated the runty little town"), the Dalhousie papers proved disappointing, and the Earl himself was a dry, unattractive figure. Almost in desperation, Creighton switched his attention to the political events which preceded the Lower

Canada Rebellion of 1837. Instead of concentrating on the French Canadian politicians, as was customary, he decided to study the period from the viewpoint of the English-speaking merchants and administrators, grouped together in the Chateau Clique. It was a characteristically obdurate decision: "I chose them purely because I wanted to be different."

Soon Creighton was struck by an awareness that the merchants were more interested in money than politics: unlike the conservative French, who were concerned with preserving a basically feudal society, the English had dreams of a huge commercial empire which would embrace the whole northern expanse of the continent. With mounting excitement, Creighton began to see a pattern that would become the basis of all his work—the existence of a vast trading network, based on the St. Lawrence River and the Great Lakes, which linked the interior of British North America to the markets of Europe. "Suddenly I realized I had an enormous and wonderful subject. I saw it extended back in the time to the start of the French regime, and forward into the future." It all fell into place one day as he was taking the train out of Ottawa, heading back to Toronto along the canal. "'West, West,' I thought, to the rhythm of the wheels. 'We're going West.' And I saw it all, in a flash. It was a moment of pure rapture." Creighton sat back in his chair, thrusting out his hands with outstretched fingers, as though to suggest the scope of his discovery. After forty years, his eyes were wide with recollected wonder.

At this point Creighton formed a close friendship with the economic historian Harold Innis, whose major study of the fur trade reinforced Creighton's own research. As Carl Berger has noted, Creighton was intrigued by Innis' conclusion that Canada became a political reality not in spite of economic laws and geography but *because* of them: "The themes that Innis had isolated—the organization of the nation around the waterways, the centralized character of

Canada's institutions, the crucial place of staple commodities, Canada's dependence on metropolitan markets, the instability and vulnerability of her economy, the North West Company as the predecessor of Canada itself—were all eventually incorporated into Creighton's own work." After exploring these themes in some early academic papers, Creighton brought them to fruition in his first book, *The Commercial Empire of the St. Lawrence, 1760-1850*, which was published in 1937. Extending Innis' economic theories into the realm of government and politics, this pioneering study traced the rise and decline of the St. Lawrence trading system from the days of the fur trade to the mid-nineteenth century, describing how a farspread business enterprise had led to the political emergence of Canada itself.

More than the personalities, it is the river itself which dominates the book and which provides the core of Creighton's vision:

> It was the one great river which led from the eastern shore into the heart of the continent. It possessed a geographical monopoly; and it shouted its uniqueness to adventurers. The river meant mobility and distance; it invited journeyings; it promised immense expanses, unfolding, flowing away into remote and changing horizons. The whole west, with all its riches, was the dominion of the river. To the unfettered and ambitious, it offered a pathway to the central mysteries of the continent. The river meant movement, transport, a ceaseless passage west and east, the long procession of river-craft—canoes, *bateaux*, timber rafts and steamboats—which followed each other into history. It seemed the destined pathway of North American trade; and from the river there rose, like an exhaltation, the dream of western commercial empire. The river was to be the basis of a great transportation system by which the manufactures

of the old world could be exchanged for the staple products of the new. This was the faith of successive generations of northerners. The dream of the commercial empire of the St. Lawrence runs like an obsession through the whole of Canadian history; and men followed each other through life, planning and toiling to achieve it. The river was not only a great actuality: it was the central truth of a religion. Men lived by it, at once consoled and inspired by its promises, its whispered suggestions, and its shouted commands; and it was a force in history, not merely because if its accomplishments, but because of its shining, ever-receding possibilities.

Here Creighton was beginning to strike those rich, majestic chords which would reverbate throughout his later work. Here, too, were the clash of personalities, the vivid details and the crisp drama which would also come to seem typically Creightonian. He would always regard history as a branch of literature. His concern with contemporary issues came relatively late in life, and had nothing to do with his original urge to become an historian. "That urge came, not from modern politics, but from English and French literature," he later wrote. "I wanted to write history for its own sake, not from the backward glance of the present, but as if what I was describing had happened the day before yesterday." According to Creighton, he was never deeply influenced by other historians. Instead it was the novelists of his youthful reading who taught him how to shape his narrative, to elucidate his characters and to recreate their circumstances. Critics would also note that Creighton's books are often constructed like plays or operas, interweaving great themes and stirring climaxes. "I adore opera, especially Wagner and Verdi," Creighton told me. "I don't much like symphonies. I like people on stage—singing to each other, in desperate circumstances."

To some academic reviewers, it was all a bit much, and even a sympathetic critic of *The Commercial Empire of the St. Lawrence* rebuked the young historian for his style: "I wish he had dipped his pen less frequently in purple ink." Forty years later, Creighton still recalled these early reviews and some of the attacks still rankled. On our last meeting, he asked me to wheel him from the living room to his study, where he pulled down a copy of his first book. "Spengler was very much in vogue when I was writing it," he said, leafing through the pages. "This last paragraph is pure Spengler — too much so — but there's an earlier bit I like." He found it quickly and began to read: " 'Two worlds lay over against each other in North America and their conflict was not only probable but certain. Between those who possessed and those who were denied the single great eastern entrance to the continent, the hostility of war could subside only into the competition of peace . . .' " Creighton closed the book. "That's pure Spengler, too," he said, shaking his head and then roaring with laughter. "There is an instinct in me for the grandiose."

Creighton's first book ends with the collapse of the old commercial empire in the mid-nineteenth century. Developing his great theme in further essays, he began to demonstrate how the business class of the two Canadas substituted economic nationalism for international commercialism. Their base was still the same — the towns and cities of the St. Lawrence — and their goal was still the exploitation of the vast northwestern regions of the continent. Instead of waterways, however, railways would become the carriers of commerce, while western settlement and protective tarriffs would foster and safeguard the growing market. At the same time, a federal union of the British North American provinces was seen as the best political protection against the expansionist threats of leading American politicians. The new Canada, in short, became a successor to the old commercial empire of the St. Lawrence.

This theme lay at the heart of Creighton's second book, *Dominion of the North*, which was published in 1944. Starting with the earliest European arrivals, and ending with the outbreak of World War Two, the book is distinctively Creightonian in its high sense of drama, its feeling for the landscape and its delight in individual characters. Largely missing, however, are the passions which came to dominate his later years. Creighton is quite explicit in maintaining that the Fathers of Confederation created a strongly centralized state, under the British Crown, as a safeguard against American annexation, and as an affirmation of British values. But he is still relatively restrained in describing the betrayal of that dream, and the book ends on a note of optimism. At that point, the United States is seen as a benevolent neighbour, rather than any sort of menace, and Creighton concludes with an affirmation of British-Canadian ties, as the two nations prepare to fight their Nazi enemy.

During the war, those views were almost universal among English Canadians, including Stephen Leacock. As an imperialist missionary, the young Leacock had argued that the United States was bent on continental hegemony, but in his later years he came to treat the great republic with jocular affection—as a rough but amiable cousin—and scornfully rejected all suggestions that it posed a threat to Canadian independence. In *While There Is Time: The Case Against Social Catastrophe*, published posthumously in 1945, Leacock wrote that there were "two fixed points, two steady beams of light" which showed Canada its postwar path. These were Canada's close links with Britain and the other Dominions, and "our firm union of friendship in mind and purpose with the United States."

Creighton echoed these views in a 1945 essay in which he emphasized Canada's historical separateness from the United States, but also wrote approvingly of their close wartime cooperation under the Joint Board of Defence. For Canada, he maintained, "friendship with the United States is the first essential of existence and the first instinct of nature." Creighton went on to state that membership in the British Commonwealth had been the second great determining factor; in the postwar world, one of Canada's major tasks would be to assist in the preservation of good Anglo-American relations.

This was an early statement of the lynch-pin theory which had become so fashionable among the mandarins in External Affairs and against which Creighton would soon be fulminating. Even in 1945, however, Creighton was privately much less sanguine about American intentions—or so he would maintain in later years. A Guggenheim fellowship took him to the United States in 1940; to that point he had little contact with anything American. In his youth, Toronto had been overwhelmingly British in its attitude and ambience, and Creighton grew up with a longing to attend an English public school. From *Little Folks* through *Boys' Own*, *Chums* and *The Scout*, he was raised on British children's weeklies and monthlies; when a boy down the street was discovered reading American comics, "we made his life miserable." Then came *The Times Weekly* and *The Times Literary Supplement*, as well as all those British and European novelists; about the only two American writers whom he read were Dreiser and Mencken. ("I liked Mencken's bellicose style, and to some extent I copied it.") Until the war, Creighton had rarely travelled to the United States and had met few Americans; now he found them insufferable. "They thought they were winning the war when they still weren't doing anything," he told me. When the Americans did enter the war after Pearl Harbour, Creighton spent the whole night lamenting the fact; later he even found himself cheering the Germans during their counter-offensive in the Ardennes. "I saw the whole future, with the Americans dominating the world. I was horrified."

With the outbreak of the Korean War, Creighton began to be more outspoken about his apprehensions. He was in Ottawa at the time, completing the first volume of his biography of Sir John A. Macdonald. Harold Innis was also in the capital, serving on a Royal Commission, and the two friends would meet for dinner in the grill room of the Chateau Laurier. Innis took an unfailing delight in the absurdities of human nature; like Creighton he rejoiced in anecdotes and acerbic comments. But their dinners became increasingly gloomy as they pondered the implications of Korea. Both men opposed Canadian participation on the United Nations side, since they saw the UN intervention as a thin disguise for American attempts to dominate the Far East. "But leading civil servants actually told us to shut up. They saw the war as some sort of holy crusade. They said we were talking heresy." Undaunted, Creighton began to write articles which advocated the peaceful acceptance of Communist regimes and which rejected as "hysterical dogmatism" the notion of a free world led by the United States. In a talk at the 1954 Couchiching Conference, he conceded that NATO had been necessary for the defence of Western Europe, but condemmed the idea that the West had a single ideology which justified intervention in Asia. "North America is not the world," he warned, "and the world will not willingly accept North American domination."

Once again Creighton was accused of heresy. John Diefenbaker, then a leading Progressive Conservative front bencher, was chairman of the session at which Creighton delivered his paper. After reading an advance copy, he told the author it was an extraordinary statement for a "Conservative historian" to make. When Creighton was finished speaking, Diefenbaker publicly rebuked him (although the Liberal Walter Gordon came up and shook his hand.) At that time, anyone who attacked the United States was regarded as at least a crypto-Communist: Creighton was denounced in the press and there were calls for his resignation from the

University of Toronto. (In fact, he was appointed chairman of the Department of History that autumn.)

Up to that point Creighton had not been actively involved in political controversy, nor — despite Diefenbaker's epithet — had he developed any partisan allegiance. Canadian federal elections failed to arouse his interest; in the one or two in which he actually voted, he cast his ballot for the Liberals and Mackenzie King. During the Depression he attended an early meeting of the League for Social Reconstruction, the group of leftist scholars and teachers who had helped form Canada's first socialist party, the CCF, but he found the session boring and never returned. "I thought my own work was more important," he recalled. Gradually, however, his own work was leading Creighton to the conviction that something had gone badly amiss with Canada, and that the culprits were the Liberal party and all its influential supporters in the civil service, the universities and the business world. His views were formed through scholarship, rather than through any instinctive political bias, and they grew out of the decade of research and writing that he devoted to Sir John A. Macdonald.

Once again Creighton found a great subject partly by chance. After completing *Dominion of the North*, he started searching for another book. His first, *The Commercial Empire of the St. Lawrence*, had the river as its main protagonist. Wanting to continue the story through the rest of the nineteenth century, he wondered whether he should adopt the CPR as his central theme. "But as they were making a nation, not just building a railway. I was fascinated by George Stephen, but I wanted more people, and an even stronger central character. Soon I found that Macdonald was behind everything. I was always driven back to him." At this point Creighton went to Innis for advice. "I told him that I wanted to do a big book and that I had two ideas — the

Anglo-French struggle in North America, and a biography of Sir John A. Innis told me 'Parkman's done the first.' That was all he said. So it was Macdonald."

Academic research is often drudgery, but in his last year Creighton would sparkle as he recalled the excitement of delving into Macdonald and his times. The trail took him to archives—in both Britain and Canada—in which he found a profusion of official papers and personal letters, especially those of Macdonald himself and the various Governors who helped him to forge the new Canadian nation. Often, in some castle or old family home, he would uncover japanned tin boxes containing bundles of fading letters tied with red ribbons. It was obvious that the bundles had not been opened for decades. In fact, much of the material had been totally neglected: soon after he began his research in 1945, Creighton was astonished to realize that there was relatively little biographical literature on Canada's first Prime Minister, and nearly all of it was relatively old. In more recent decades, Canadian historians had either ignored Macdonald or else they had portrayed him as "Old Tomorrow"—a procrastinating, drunken schemer who was devoid of convictions and none too scrupulous in his intrigues. In a paper delivered in 1947, Creighton gave a tentative explanation of these omissions and distortions. He charged that his fellow historians had become preoccupied with interpreting Canadian development as a struggle for emancipation from Britain, overlooking both London's enthusiastic support of Confederation and the constant threat to British North America from the United States. They had set out, he said with heavy irony, "to rescue Canada from the discredit of its all too British past and to rehabilitate it as a decent American community." Since Macdonald had based his policy on maintaining the Anglo-Canadian alliance as a safeguard against American incursions, then Macdonald was a heretic to be dismissed with casual contempt.

By 1957, when his two volumes were at last completed and published, Creighton became even more specific in his attack. In a lecture at Carleton University, he maintained that Macdonald's real crime was his failure to conform to what Creighton was now calling the Authorized Version of Canadian history. This was the creed that declared that Canada was the outcome of an encounter between the forces of nationality and British imperialism, and that its inevitable destiny was an even closer alliance with the United States. Creighton now named Mackenzie King and his advisors as the chief proponents and beneficiaries of this approach: "In Canada it is not necessarily assumed that historical truth is to be found in a comprehensive and careful investigation of the evidence of archives, libraries and men's memories. Historical truth is laid up, a priceless and absolutely untouchable deposit, in the private minds of Liberal politicians, Liberal civil servants, Liberal journalists and Liberal historians. And as the Liberal government in Canada has gone on from strength to strength and decade to decade, the majestic orthodoxy of the Authorized Version has grown."

There was no such direct attack in the books themselves: *John A. Macdonald: The Young Politician* (1952) and *John A. Macdonald: The Old Chieftain* (1955). Rather than looking back on events with hindsight, Creighton told his story with drama, building from one climax to another and concentrating on the feel of the actual historical moment. In the process, however, the biography was a massive refutation of the Authorized Version. Time and time again, Creighton underlined Macdonald's vision of Confederation; moreover, in presenting Macdonald as a statesman who *had* a vision, and who finally achieved it, Creighton rescued our first Prime Minister from the neglect or calumny which had long been his lot at the hands of other historians.

The biography was widely hailed as a scholarly and artistic masterpiece, rich with fresh insights and original research, and epic in its portrayal of the central character.

Each volume won a Governor General's Literary Award; together they were seen as setting new standards in Canadian biography. But not everyone was completely won over. There were complaints that Creighton, by seeing the whole course of events exclusively through the eyes of his hero, had made Macdonald into a giant among pygmies. It was noted that he had used every ounce of his literary abilities to underline the contrast: according to Frank Underhill, a colleague and ideological rival at the University of Toronto, the biography would have been more impressive if only "those political leaders who collided with Macdonald were not only intellectually deficient and morally delinquent but also physically repulsive."

Once the biography was completed, Creighton was quick to point out its contemporary relevance. In his 1957 paper, he held that Macdonald's career was "a tract for the times" since it showed Canadians that there was a legitimate historical basis for a much more vigorous and independent foreign policy. "Macdonald's prime purpose," he wrote, "was to found a transcontinental nation which would have a separate and autonomous existence in North America. His fundamental aim was to protect Canada from the dangers of continentalism; and it is the dangers of continentalism, economic, political and military, which now seem to be pressing in upon us steadily and from every side." Canadians, he added, were entering "the most exciting and dangerous period in their political existence."

Creighton was now at the crossroads of his earlier optimism and the angry despair which would mark his last years. There *were* grounds for optimism in 1957. In that year, Creighton also wrote a new final chapter for the revised edition of *Dominion of the North*, in which he cited the Massey Report, the Canada Council and the strong work by artists in every field as signs that Canadians might be forging a new sense of their national identity. Two years later, in *The Story of Canada*, a short history for the general reader, he wrote that Canadians might even be entering a new Elizabethan era.

One major reason for optimism was the Conservative victories of 1957 and 1958 which ended two decades of Liberal rule and gave John Diefenbaker a massive majority in the House of Commons. Back in 1945, when he was starting his research on Macdonald, Creighton had attended an election night party in Ottawa. The room was crowded with civil servants who cheered and toasted Mackenzie King's victory at the polls. Creighton was appalled that the bureaucrats were so partisan. "I thought—'My God—these guys are going to govern the country—for years and years!'" Now, after Liberal arrogance had reached its apogee in the pipeline debate, the Grits had finally been turned out, and Creighton concluded his 1959 book by asserting that the Conservatives had politically reunited the Canadian nation. (In a last flurry of optimistic rhetoric, Roy Faibish, one of the young Tory advisors from western Canada, had drawn upon William Arthur Deacon's 1933 book when he wrote the speech with which Diefenbaker launched his triumphant campaign.)

Nor was Creighton alone in his hopes and concerns. Innis was dead, but other intellectual allies had come to the fore, among them the western historian W. L. Morton, the constitutional expert Eugene Forsey, the young philosopher George Grant, the journalist Judith Robinson and the scholar John Farthing. These thinkers differed among themselves on a host of subjects, and never became a formal cabal, but they all agreed that the long years of Liberal rule had seriously eroded Canadian independence and Canadian parliamentary traditions. They also wrote like vengeful angels. One of their most notable productions was *Freedom Wears a Crown*, a series of essays which Farthing wrote before his death in 1954, and which was edited by Judith Robinson for publication in 1957. More than just a defence of the

monarchy, it was also a blistering indictment of the Authorized Version. As a young man, Farthing had been one of
Leacock's associates at McGill; in these last essays, he attacked
the Liberal view of Canada's destiny with an acerbity as
strong as anything in Creighton. The Liberals, he wrote, *had*
no positive ideal of national life. French Canadians were to
retain their cultural heritage intact, while the rest were to
adjust to whatever demands were made upon them in the
name of national unity:

> Having erased our past, as a dark period of
> serfdom under an imperialist yoke; and some-
> thing therefore to be forgotten and destroyed;
> having denied the historical tradition in which
> our life as a people is rooted, we have nothing
> remaining but the future to which we can appeal;
> the dream of an ever-increasing forest of smoke
> stacks.

This, of course, was also Creighton's main concern. In a
speech at Trent University in 1965, he warned that "A nation
that repudiates or distorts its past runs a great danger of
forfeiting its future." His own career had been devoted to
re-establishing the authentic Canadian tradition of Macdonald, and to refuting the distortions of the Authorized Version. In the late nineteen-fifties, Creighton had felt reasonably
hopeful that Canadians were paying heed, and might renew
their sense of national purpose. By the end of the decade,
however, his optimism was on the wane. In 1964 he published *The Road to Confederation: The Emergence of Canada,
1863-1867.* This richly detailed and dramatic account built on
all his previous work, but there was also a new and dis-
quieted tone. In his earlier books, Creighton had held that
economics made Confederation inevitable; now he saw the
union as a chancier achievement, even as something brought
about mainly by diplomacy and political cunning. As
Michael Cross noted, this transition in Creighton's thought

showed "a profound loss of optimism in the certainty of Canadian success."

There were immediate reasons for Creighton's pessimism. The flounderings of the Diefenbaker government dismayed all those who had looked to the Conservatives to turn the tide of continentalism—in his sombre *Lament for a Nation* (1965), George Grant wrote that "The 1957 election was the Canadian people's last gasp of nationalism. Diefenbaker's government was the strident swan-song of that hope." Even before then, the Suez crisis had shattered any remaining illusions about British power and Commonwealth solidarity: in a world increasingly divided between the American and Soviet empires, there was no longer any practical prospect of using the Anglo-Canadian alliance to offset American pressures. In a paper delivered in 1969, Creighton noted gloomily that no Canadian political party had drawn up a comprehensive program for the defence of Canadian political and economic independence, "and only a few individuals—a Governor of the Bank of Canada, a Conservative Prime Minister, a Liberal Minister of Finance, and a few university professors—have ever urged that there was a real danger which must be met, if Canada wished to survive." Since the defence agreements of 1940, Canada had been exposed to the irresistible penetrative power of American economic and military imperialism. Citing the 1963 crisis over nuclear warheads on Canadian soil, Creighton said that the real leader of the Liberal party during that period was not Lester B. Pearson but John F. Kennedy, and that it was American pressures which probably contributed most to the downfall of Diefenbaker: "About the only manifestation of American power which was spared Canada in the crisis was the sight of American tanks rumbling up Parliament Hill in Ottawa. But the Canadians, unlike the Czechs, who are a brave and independent people, do not need tanks to coerce them. All they require is the instructions of an American President, an American Secretary of State, and an American general as to where their best interests lie. Then, dutifully, they act accordingly." Reviewing all the evidence of American domination, Creighton concluded sorrowfully that the trend "is now probably irreversible."

There were two other major reasons for Creighton's pessimism: like continentalism, they also derived from the rewriting of history and the actions of Liberal governments. His studies convinced him that the Fathers of Confederation had designed a great transcontinental nation; because French Canada wished to preserve its distinctive culture with some measure of local autonomy, this union had to be a federal one. But the Fathers were dismayed by the spectacle of the United States, immersed in a horrendous civil war partly because of the powers granted by the American Constitution to individual states; including the Quebec delegates, they determined to create the most strongly *centralized* union that was possible under federal forms. To Creighton, this was the clear intention of the British North America Act, but since 1867 the original vision had been steadily eroded. The process had begun with key decisions by the courts, especially the Judicial Committee of the Privy Council, which transferred significant powers to the provinces. Then the politicians took over. During the Depression and World War Two, the Dominion government still maintained its economic and financial control. After the war, however, provincial pressures and federal concessions had increasingly transferred revenues and powers to the provinces. In 1965, Creighton warned prophetically: "This huge increase in the provincial share of the public or government sector of the economy could threaten serious trouble for the future." (By the nineteen-eighties, of course, disputes between Ottawa and the provinces *had* created a recurring crisis which not even the new constitution seemed likely to alleviate.)

But it was the situation in Quebec which aroused Creighton's deeper ire and even stronger forebodings. Again he returned to the Confederation period to argue that the

Fathers had given official recognition to the French language only within the narrowest of limits. Although he supported the preservation of a distinctive French culture, he strongly attacked the idea of special status for Quebec, and dismissed as historically false the notion that Confederation had been based on any bicultural compact. As the Quiet Revolution gained ground in the nineteen-sixties, Creighton lashed out against both its leaders in Quebec and its sympathizers in English Canada, including some of his fellow historians. The former were distorting history to support their claims for special status; the latter were simple, gullible and ignorant. "No moral commitment has been dishonoured and no contract broken," Creighton argued in 1966, "there is no reason for a sense of guilt and no case for making amends. The simple truth is that French Canada and the Province of Quebec have not got less than they were promised in 1867; they have, in fact, been given infinitely more."

When the Parti Quebecois won power in 1976, unveiled its language legislation and promised a referendum on separation, Creighton again roared to the attack with a passionate article in *Maclean's*. For English Canada, he argued, the politics of appeasement had become bankrupt and "the policies of self-defense and self-preservation must take their place." English Canada should accept separation only if Quebec left Confederation as it entered it, minus the vast and rich northern area of Ungava, as well as Labrador, which had been awarded to Newfoundland in 1927. Canada would have to insist on all its rights to the St. Lawrence Seaway, possibly by establishing a protective zone for five miles on either side of the waterway. Since Quebec was rejecting bilingualism for unilingualism, English Canada's whole bilingual program, which never had any constitutional or cultural justification, had ceased to have any political purpose, and should be scrapped. There could be no question of a customs union after separation; once Canada imposed its tariff wall against Quebec, "René Lévesque, his associates and his deluded followers will be left to themselves in the stagnant economic backwater of independence."

This article disturbed me at the time, and Creighton's attitude to Quebec continued to trouble me throughout our conversations. It might well be that the French Canadian nationalists and their English Canadian sympathizers were guilty of revisionism, but Creighton's attitude seemed excessively harsh. It was, I suspected, part of a weakness in the outlook of many conservatives, especially older ones—in adopting their own nationalist stance, they tended to stress the Britishness of Canada to an extent that offered little place to their French-speaking compatriots. This seemed counter-productive—to put it mildly—and I doubted whether Creighton's exemplary conservative would have gone so far. Indeed Macdonald—for all that he was castigated in Quebec for approving the execution of Riel—had often supported French language rights outside the province. As he told the House of Commons in 1890: "I have no accord with the desire expressed in some quarters that by any mode whatever there should be any attempt made to oppress the one language or render it inferior to the other; I believe it would be impossible if it were tried, and that it would be foolish and wicked if it were possible."

Creighton's views on Quebec aroused great controversy. They also dismayed many of his friends, and involved him in semi-public rows with George Grant and W. L. Morton. Clearly he had a distrust of French Canadians, although his prejudice seemed based on historical study rather than direct acquaintance. In one of his books, French Canadians are described as "sullen, suspicious, unresponsive"; elsewhere he condemns their "narrow professional education, unenterprising capitalists and their venal and obscurantist politicians." Too often, it seemed, Creighton misapplied those historical strictures to a contemporary Quebec which was bursting with enterprise and new ideas. What he really hated about the French Canadians, however, was not their Frenchness, but their repeated attempts to destroy Macdonald's great nation. As he wrote in 1971, continentalism was the strongest opponent of Canadian nationalism, but "continentalism is merely the upper millstone; the lower millstone, parochialism or provincialism, is its complement; and it is the attrition by these two powerful forces that has ground down the solid fabric of Canadian nationalism." In 1970, Creighton had published *Canada's First Century*. Unlike his earlier books, this is a solemn, even tragic account, totally lacking any of the euphoria with which so many Canadians had greeted their nation's centennial. In the final chapter—"Epilogue: Ottawa, 1967"—Creighton described all those factors which were eroding Canadian unity and independence, and concluded that the battle was virtually lost.

Canada's First Century was Creighton's last major work. In 1976, as part of the Canadian Centenary Series, he published *The Forked Road: Canada, 1939-1957*. Ostensibly a survey of the period, the book turned into a sustained polemic on how the Liberals sold out the country to the Americans. As Creighton piles on the evidence, his exasperation is palpable; even sympathetic critics noted that the book suffered from his heavy-handed approach.

Then, in 1978, with his body failing but his mind still alert, Creighton surprised just about everyone by producing a novel. It was not his first attempt. As a young professor in the nineteen-thirties, he had tried his hand at fiction— mysteries in the vein of Conan Doyle and humour in the style of P. G. Wodehouse—but these came to nothing. Which is probably just as well: even allowing for the age of the author, there is little in *Takeover* to suggest that Creighton had missed his true vocation. But the novel does entertain, with its sharp observations of Toronto, its grim ironies and its frequent high spirits. ("Writing it was tremendous fun," Creighton told me.) This gaiety is somewhat startling, for Creighton's subject—the attempted takeover by Americans of an old Canadian firm—is an obvious metaphor for his darkening apprehensions about the fate of the whole nation. In the end, however, the takeover is apparently averted; the means are melodramatic, but there is a clear suggestion that the weight of historic tradition has triumphed over modern greed. Thwarted in his plans to sell out, the head of the old Canadian family is left to ponder his dilemma: "He had tried to escape from the past—tried with all his strength and ingenuity. But the past had reached out and clutched him, and held him fast."

After Creighton's death, some commentators seized upon that passage as his epitaph, suggesting that the historian had never come to terms with the twentieth century, and that his work had suffered through his passionate identification with Macdonald and his dream. These verdicts riled me: they seemed part of the customary liberal denigration of any tory vision, that dogged attempt to deny our particular traditions and to transform us into second-class Americans. Or were they simply realistic? Was Creighton's vision doomed, as he himself suggested? Was there nothing left of the conservative tradition but the memory of an old man raging against the dark, and a shelf of magnificent books?

Again I had a stubborn instinct that such was not the case. By now, however, I had to acknowledge a distinct unease. It was something I had often felt when reading Creighton, or listening to him. There were so many areas in which he sounded like a reactionary old curmudgeon. This was part of his charm, of course, as well as the effusion of his passion, but it hardly inspired confidence in his relevance.

I found it easy to embrace Creighton's vision of a strong transcontinental nation, steeped in British traditions, which offered a distinct alternative to the liberal republicanism of the United States. But I was troubled by his centralist bias, and especially his lack of sympathy for French Canadian and Western aspirations. The rights of *any* minority—and human rights in general—were hardly a prominent concern with Creighton, nor did he have much to say about the role of socialist and other reform movements. Almost single-handedly, Creighton had rehabilitated Macdonald and reasserted the conservative tradition as our dominant historical force, but that no longer seemed enough to heal our present wounds. It was necessary as a starting point, but hardly sufficient as a solution.

So I was left with the dilemma: was there any form of conservatism which made sense in our modern era? If so, it would have to encompass those areas in which Creighton's vision seemed most vulnerable. At that point, I suspected there were aspects of the tradition, still potent, which Creighton had neglected and which might be relevant. At that point, too, I recalled Creighton's own account of how his vision came to him. And so I headed West.

III
Western Loyalties:
W. L. Morton

Over the years I had seen something of the West without coming to know it. Mainly I had seen its cities, and my most vivid memory was of walking around the centre of Calgary, where whole blocks had been razed, and dozens of new skyscrapers were rising amid a forest of cranes. Not surprisingly it struck me that a city which could so brazenly uproot its core had scant sense of its heritage. This fitted with other images derived from my reading—images of fabulous wealth and aggressive expansion, of blue-eyed sheikhs and tough-talking entrepreneurs. These impressions were superficial, but they made me skeptical about the nature of Western conservatism. Whatever I was searching out, it wasn't a rough-and-ready capitalism which seemed more American than Canadian in its inspiration. Nor did western Conservative politicians like Peter Lougheed appear to be motivated by any doctrine more appealing than expediency, while Joe Clark—during his brief tenure as Prime

Minister—had failed notably to give new life to the tory tradition. At this stage I was groping, without any clear sense of what the West might have to offer. Yet I had been told there *was* a Western conservatism which had deep roots and a different flavour from that of Creighton's anglo-toryism. And so I went to Winnipeg, to meet its most notable exponent.

William Morton was a big man, with broad shoulders and a powerful frame. His face was tanned and rugged, with a strong lower lip and a firm jaw. When I first saw him, waiting for me at the Winnipeg airport, he was wearing a white-and-brown checked jacket and brown slacks. For a distinguished scholar in his seventies, he looked distinctly dapper, although I also sensed his dignity. There was something measured and deliberate about Morton—the way he spoke and the way he moved—something that seemed more rural than academic. Something of the yeoman. In the parking lot, when I remarked upon the brilliant spring-time sky, he gave my banal comment a moment of consideration, before replying gravely that the farmer in him had to be apprehensive, since the land was much too dry. Later I found this passage in one of his essays:

> The walking plough, tipped with its point set to slip into the sod, its mouldboard gleaming a lambent silver polished by miles of turning soil, jerks as the horses lean into the collars, and the furrow rolls.

> Such is one of the clearest images of my boyhood memory. It is an image drawn from one of the many skills of old-time farming, the breaking every July of a few acres of more new land from meadow and poplar bush. I look back on it with fondness for something gone forever except in

fading memory, and am proud that I was once good at the plough.

Pride in his roots and pride in his province—both were still evident. As Morton drove me into town—gingerly manoeuvering his small Honda through the mid-morning traffic—I told him I knew very little about Manitoba. "Yes," he answered drily. "When people talk about 'the West' these days, they mean Saskatchewan, Alberta and B. C. Because they have the resources. But Manitoba—this is where it all *began!*"

Suddenly I caught a glimpse of a most astonishing structure—a palatial, high-domed building which sprawled across the centre of a vast park. Grandiose and opulent, it had towering pillars and a magnificent portico. Somehow I had a fleeting sense of Buckingham Palace *and* St. Paul's Cathedral. I knew this had to be the Legislature, but I was startled to find something so imperious at the gateway to the West. Whatever was it doing here, and whose were all those statues, placed so stolidly around the park, like a procession of Roman Emperors? Before I could question Morton about them, we were drawing up to my hotel, and he was saying he was pleased I had picked the Fort Garry in preference to the newer, slicker hostelries. With quiet pride he informed me that when the Fort Garry was renovated, he was asked to name the main restaurant. In deference to the decades when the territory was ruled by the Hudson's Bay Company, he chose to call it The Factor's Table.

Morton lived with his wife not far from the hotel—on the tenth floor of an apartment building just across the Assiniboine River from the Legislature. The living room was dominated by a large oil painting of a young woman: Morton told me it was his wife's great-grandmother: "There's a rumour that Sir John A. almost made her his second wife." This came out casually, and yet I somehow felt that I was being introduced to the lady! So far my whole reception had been casual (as well as courteous), but now I was starting to sense a deeper formality in Morton, an underlying *gravitas*. Then, as we sat down, Morton suggested that he should start by discussing his parents. At that point I remembered something Creighton had said, something about Canadians lacking any sense of lineage. And I recalled that Morton, in one of his essays, had written that a concern for ancestors and antecedents was one of the distinguishing marks of a conservative: "He is interested in family; he instinctively wants to know who your people were and where you came from."

Morton was the third generation to plough the family land. Of English and Scottish stock, he grew up in a log house, a pioneer dwelling which his grandfather had built in the eighteen-seventies. At that time, between the two Riel rebellions, Manitoba had just become a province of the new Dominion. When Morton was born in 1908, Riel was long since hanged, and the Métis and the original British immigrants had been overwhelmed by an influx of settlers from Ontario, as well as thousands more from the Ukraine and other parts of central Europe. As Morton later wrote, Manitoba was set on its path to be a crucible of Canadian nationalism.

Yet the early influences were strongly imperial, reflecting the importance of Selkirk's settlement and the long dominance of the Hudson's Bay Company. Like Creighton's Toronto, Morton's boyhood Manitoba was a very British world. Everything in the house—the tea caddies, the dishes, the jackknives, the best boots, the heaviest coats and the finest hats—all were British-made, while the yearly calendars pictured an heroic lion or an intimidating battleship. The King's portrait hung on the wall of the schoolhouse, and Morton's favourite exercise book had a cover showing in colour the death of Brock.

Life on the pioneer farm was harsh, but not devoid of culture. There were books in the home, and after chores were done, the young Morton read them avidly, as well as scouting more volumes in the homes of neighbours. ("So I hunted books as I hunted partridge and rabbits," he later wrote, "with the same care and pleasure in the kill. After having read and reread all the books to hand, to get a new book was to feel the same fierce pleasure as to bring down a duck on the wing.") Like Creighton, Morton progressed from *Mother Goose* and the *Boy's Own Annual* to Dickens and Burns, as well as the Victorian sagas of travel and adventure. This eclectic reading served to release the farm boy from the landscape over which he toiled, opening his eyes to broader perspectives. Something was stirring in Morton—an urge to write—although it would be many years before he could reconcile the actual and the literary landscapes. He would never be aroused by the literature of cities; instead he was stirred by the example of Burns, setting his poetry amid his local Ayrshire: "A challenge had emerged. If Burns could sing of Sweet Afton, why not I, or another, of the local stream, the Whitemud? But it was a daunting thought; the Whitemud, even when it ran clear in early summer, ran through raw clay banks, and in any case nobody had ever heard of it."

At first it seemed the land might hold him fast. He intended to be a farmer; when he had trouble with maths in high school, he dropped out for two years to work on the family farm. "But when I saw I was only to be my father's hired hand, I went on to the University of Manitoba to sort things out." Again like Creighton, he was drawn to literature, and thought of doing a Ph.D. on Hardy. At the same time, his writing for *The Manitoban* drew him to the attention of J. W. Dafoe, the powerful editor of *The Winnipeg Free Press*, who urged him to pursue a career in journalism. When a Rhodes Scholarship took him to Oxford in 1932, however, Morton turned towards history. "This was in the Depression," he recalled, "but it wasn't a case of an academic career offering better opportunities. I knew I could always get a job on the *Free Press*. I think I became fascinated by historical research — nothing deeper."

Morton returned to Winnipeg in 1935: for the next thirty years he would be associated with the University of Manitoba, eventually as head of its history department. From the start he was drawn to the history of his native province and, in particular, its pioneer settlements. Yet his viewpoint was never parochial: in his first book, *Third Crossing* (1946), which studied the district around his home-town of Gladstone, he explicitly viewed the small settlement as an outpost of empire which had been founded by people steeped in the civilized values of Western Europe, and especially the British Isles. Increasingly he would insist that Manitoba's history had *not* begun in 1870, that it went back to the Elizabethan explorers and the French fur traders, that it included Selkirk's colony and the Red River settlement.

Increasingly, too, this broad outlook made Morton attack the Laurentian thesis of Innis and Creighton — not for any inaccuracies, but for its centralist bias. In 1946, he published a paper in which he asserted that the Laurentian theme was too narrowly economic, and that it paid scant attention to the aspirations of the West, or to the need to establish just relations between the different regions and races. Condemning Eastern "aggression" he wrote that the West was annexed to Confederation as a subordinate region and had so remained for sixty years. "For Confederation was brought about to increase the wealth of central Canada, and until the original purpose is altered, and the concentration of wealth and population by national policy in central Canada ceases, Confederation will remain an instrument of injustice."

With growing eloquence, Morton would continue to espouse the view that Canada could survive only through the recognition of legitimate regional differences. In his next book, *Progressive Party in Canada* (1950), he traced the rise and fall of the agrarian protest movement of the nineteen-twenties. In a 1955 essay, he noted that central Canadian institutions and ideals had long since prevailed in the West, but that the tradition of prairie grievance and utopian politics had sprung from the subordinate status given to the West in Confederation. Then, in 1957, Morton published his major work, *Manitoba: A History*. Writing with a verve and an emotional commitment which rivalled Creighton's, he described his province's long history and its complex heritage of British, French and other European strains. This was not a separatist tract, but a proud celebration of Manitoba as a distinctive region within the larger Canadian community. It was also a paean to the fortitude of a people who had triumphed over a grim environment and who had remained faithful to the civilized traditions of their European ancestors:

> ... Manitobans had been made, as Canadians had been made, of those who by endurance in loyalty to older values than prosperity, had learned to wrest a living from the prairie's brief summer and the harsh rocks and wild waters of the north. Manitoba, like Canada, was the response to the challenge of the north, a challenge not quickly nor easily met. And those who remained and met that challenge, generation on generation, might hope to see in the life of their country, by work of hand or word of spirit, some stubborn northern flowering.

By now I was beginning to understand the depth of Morton's pride in his roots. By now, too, I was becoming less skeptical about the relevance of Western conservatism. True, I was talking to Morton at a time — the spring of 1980 — when regional jealousies were proclaimed in strident tones, and when I felt an uncharacteristic sympathy for Pierre Trudeau in his attempt to retain some semblance of a nation. Although

I had little use for the Lévesques and the Lougheeds, however, I was moved by Morton's championing of a distinctive Western experience; I was also starting to believe that Creighton *had* been overly centralist.

It was, of course, a matter of balance—a balance which Morton himself was careful to establish when he switched to more national themes in the nineteen-sixties. This was a gradual evolution, and it implied no weakening of Morton's sense of roots. His writing would always be marked by his youthful experience of a harsh northern landscape, and by his sympathy for the rights of different regions and different races. But in his major works of this period—*The Canadian Identity* (1961), *The Kingdom of Canada* (1963) and *The Critical Years the Union of British North America, 1857-1873* (1964)— Morton presented a conservative and nationalist vision of Canada which had striking similarities to that of Creighton.

It was a vision which accepted the Laurentian theme as a true account of the Dominion's origins and of its historic dependence—both economic and military—on external powers. It was a vision which also stressed the unity of Canada, and a national identity which embraced not only the two founding races but also the later immigrant groups. "By Canadian history also it is to be understood not one French and one British, but the entire history of all Canada. There are not two histories, but one history, as there are not two Canadas, or any greater number, but only one. Nor are there two ways of life, but one common response to land and history expressed in many strong variants of the one, it is true, but still one central substance."

This "central substance" was markedly different to that of the United States. For Morton, Canada was distinguished by its northern character and its European roots, especially its adherence to British traditions. To cope with the harsh geography and the inhospitable climate, governments and communities had taken the lead in fostering social and economic development. Canada was therefore inherently conservative, stressing the mutual obligations of all citizens within an organic society, and rejecting the liberal individualism of the American revolutionaries. Instead of severing their roots, Canadians had elected to build on those traditions, including allegiance to the monarchy, in order to fulfil a particular destiny:

> Not life, liberty and the pursuit of happiness, but peace, order and good government are what the national government of Canada guarantees. Under these it is assumed life, liberty and happiness may be achieved, but each according to his taste. For a society of allegiance admits of a diversity the society of compact does not, and one of the blessings of the Canadian way of life is that there is no Canadian way of life, much less two, but a unity under the crown admitting a thousand diversities.

In emphasizing the importance of the monarchy, Morton made clear that he was advocating neither "a sentimental royalism" nor "the regrettable Edwardian pomp which alienated the affections of so many Canadians from the outward expression of what is the core of the Canadian political tradition." Rather, he was describing a set of constitutional principles which were the best guarantee that Canadians would remain free under the rule of law, with full scope for all their differences, rather than becoming subject to the levelling and conformist pressures of republican rule. "In Canada, a country of economic hazard, external dependence, and plural culture, only the objective reality of a monarchy and the permanent force of monarchial institutions could form the centre and pivot of unity. Allegiance was a social and political necessity of national existence and prevailed over the manifest and insistent attractions of republican institutions and republican liberty."

Again, this made a lot of sense to me. My own background was staunchly monarchist and anglophile, but I was too much of a Canadian to subscribe to what Leacock called "a truckling subservience to English people and English ideas"—especially when both the people and the ideas had a contemporary manifestation which was often not only arrogant, but also second-rate. Like many Canadians, I loved my British heritage, but also resented it. So I was in tune with Morton when he made clear that he was advocating a conservative and monarchial approach for solid historical and political reasons, and not because he was merely a sentimental anglophile. In a moving address to students in 1964, Morton described his boyhood in rural Manitoba and how he grew up in that very British world. Like Leacock and the other Ontario Imperialists of the time, however, Manitobans were saved from being complete colonials through also having a strong sense of being Canadian. "The English Canadian is American, Scots, Irish, or northern English by origin, to a far greater degree than he is southern or dominant English," Morton said. "Like those people, he dislikes the southern English, bickers with them, and joins them only in the face of external attack. Our Britishness, then, was not Englishness, but a local brew of our own which we called Canadian."

At the same time, however, Morton had taken great pride in his Britishness—a pride which he now admitted had a selfish aspect. "It was an advantage to be British a generation ago as it is something extra to be American today." Like Leacock, too, he had been slow to recognize the steady decline in British power and the growing insignificance for Canadians of the British Empire (as opposed to British institutions). As he told the students, the crucial realization had come to him only the previous year, when the Pearson government adopted the new Canadian flag, an emblem devoid of any historic and especially British connotations: "I have, in short, become aware over the past few months—I wonder at how stupidly and belatedly—that a prestige that I once unconsciously possessed I now have consciously not got. I have become Canadian like any other, a member of an ethnic minority, and am obliged to make such way in the world as my personal merit permits." While this might be the cause of regret (Morton referred in passing to "the world I lost last spring"), it seems to have liberated him to an even greater awareness of the potential which resided in a Canada of many races. Again to the students, he spoke about their country's destiny in language which recalled the earlier effusions of Leacock, Sandwell and Deacon:

> We Canadians — English Canadians, French Canadians, German Canadians, Ukrainian Canadians, Italian Canadians — of whatever origin we are, whatever culture we cherish, whatever language we speak, all of us with no exception whatever, are called to greatness. We are called by the unique nature of the Canadian community, a political community without nationalism or ideology, a community of political allegiance alone. We are called to greatness together, all of us, with no one hanging back, no one contracting out, no one relying on an ultimate deal with the United States. We have in fact no choice. If we are to be Canadian, we must be so together, because in fragments we shall be drawn into the United States by affinities of taste and the imperatives of defence, and lose all the word Canadian now means to us. The observation is not restricted to the old French, or the old American, or the old British stock. It applies to all of us and has no meaning apart from all of us.

This was part of what Morton was calling — with increasing emphasis — the "moral purpose" of the Canadian community. He now saw Confederation as something much greater than a product of economic necessity and practical politics. For a start, the Canadian experiment, through the extension of responsible government into independent nationhood, had established a non-revolutionary pattern for the post-colonial world, especially the Commonwealth. ("That what was worked out on the banks of the St. Lawrence and the shores of Lake Ontario should have helped, however remotely, to bring into being great new states of free and sovereign communities on the banks of the Ganges and Indus and on the coasts of West and East Africa, constitutes Canada's single but significant contribution to the slow elaboration of human freedom.") The history of Canada, he added, had universal significance because Canadians had demonstrated the importance, and the possibility, of enduring in the face of a menacing landscape, beside a much larger and often hostile neighbour, while maintaining a delicate balance between their individual freedoms and their collective responsibility for the freedom and welfare of all their fellow citizens:

> The preservation of such a national society is not the unique mission of Canada, but it is the central fact of Canadian history that it has been preserved and elaborated by Canadians in one of the largest, harshest and most intimidating countries on earth. Canada, that is, has preserved and confirmed the essentials of the greatest of civilizations in the grimmest of environments. It is an accomplishment worthy of a better end than absorption in another and alien society, however friendly and however strong in its own ideals. In that accomplishment and its continuence lies the relevance of Canadian history.

Those words had stirred me when I read them for the first time: they stirred me again when I reread them on the plane to Winnipeg. It seemed that Morton had gone beyond Creighton—in that he had opened up aspects of the Canadian experience which Creighton tended to ignore. Like Creighton, he articulated a vision of Canada which was conservative and based on British traditions. With Morton there was also a firm sense of the northern landscape and a strong concern for the dignity and rights of different regions and racial groups. Canada, in short, was based on a balance between cultural diversity and allegiance to a shared political community.

This last seemed especially crucial: it occurred to me that racial equality was not only a genuine conservative ideal; it had even found a place in the policies of the Conservative party. I recalled Diefenbaker's passionate admonitions on the subject, a stance which grew legitimately out of the slights he had suffered because of his Germanic name. And I remembered a conversation with his External Affairs minister, that fervent anglophile Howard Green, who used to call his ambassadors "my boys" and who told me he had just appointed "my first Icelandic boy". Then there was Joe Clark's cabinet, in which a MacDonald and a Macdonald were balanced by a Hnatyshyn and a Mazankowski. While the Liberal party had always been successful in manipulating the so-called ethnic vote, the Conservatives—at their best—had not shirked from practising the openness which Morton preached.

I also had a sense of personal liberation. For Morton was countering the widespread view that the archetypal Canadian conservative is a Bay Street businessman of English or Scottish origin whose natural habitat also includes the Turf Club at Woodbine and the best boxes at the Royal Winter Fair. Since I came out of that precise milieu, and flattered myself that my inclinations to piratical free enterprise and social snobbery were less than rampant, I was sensitive about the stereotype; I also knew that the bland, smug rulers of my native province (by the early nineteen-eighties, they had taken on the lineaments of an unshakable dynasty) were not my kind of tories. With Morton, it seemed that I was on the track of a conservatism which was decent, compassionate and open to the complexities of Canadian life.

Yet after my first few hours with Morton, I was discomfited and almost downcast. Perhaps I had been spoiled by Creighton, with all his passion. Perhaps I expected that Morton would be as epic in person as he was with his pen. Instead I encountered a man who was not only laconic in his speech and subdued in his gestures (Creighton used his arms like scimitars; Morton tended to clasp his hands together), but who also seemed bemused when I quoted some of his most fervent statements. When I mentioned his 1964 address, and in particular his sorrowful reference to "the world I lost last spring", Morton was nonplussed and said he couldn't recall exactly what he had meant. "It was probably the flag," he finally ventured. "I was very angry about that...leaving out all tradition . . . " Then his voice trailed off and he failed to elaborate. (Creighton had roared a sermon on the subject.) When I asked Morton about his striking assertion of Canada's "moral purpose", he seemed anxious to avoid any inflationary misconception: "I guess I meant the rule of law . . . not much more than that. These things *do* have a moral purpose . . . decency in politics and that sort of thing . . . " Again the voice trailed off. Apparently it was Morton's nature to be modest and reticent; he was also in declining health. (He would die within the year — on December 6, 1980, at the age of 71.) But I missed the passion that was in his prose. There was still some connection to be made: I sensed this was a connection not so much between the man and his writing, as between the writer and his habitat. At this point, sitting in that high-rise apartment, I lacked the correlative that I had found between Creighton and his home and street in Brooklin, or Leacock and his house on Old Brewery Bay: a sense of placement. Wonderfully, however, that was soon to come.

Taking a break from our discussions, I wander back to my hotel through the grounds of the Legislature. Now I can inspect more closely that remarkable building which first caught my eye through the window of Morton's Honda. My God, it *is* stupendous! Towering above the trees, it's Buckingham Palace *surmounted* by St. Paul's Cathedral. I think of my own Queen's Park . . . I've always found it handsome and distinguished . . . but in comparison to *this*, Queen's Park is little more than a pretentious brick warehouse. How on earth does one explain such opulence? I wonder if my guide book can help. But it tells me only that when the building was planned just after the turn of the century, the legislators were unanimous in their desire to erect "an imposing structure". That's evident enough, and hardly helps. Now my eye rises up along the massive pillars, along the curved blue dome, to encounter a gleaming statue at the very top, a graceful figure reaching out into the sparkling sky. This, my guide book states, is the Golden Boy: " . . . probably Manitoba's best known symbol . . . . . He faces the north, with its mineral resources, fish, forest, furs, water power and seaport, where his province's future lies." It occurs to me that the Boy is also showing his bare buttocks to the south, where the Great Republic lies.

Dazed by all this grandeur, I wander around the side of the Legislature where I find another building which is much smaller, but equally elegant. This is a three-storey, white-brick mansion with an implacable central tower and a blue mansard roof. Highest of all, rising from the top of the tower, there's a flag staff with a Union Jack encompassing what must be the Manitoban coat of arms. Once more I plunge into my guide book . . . it assures me that I'm contemplating Government House, official residence of the Lieutenant-Governor. That's all it tells me, and again it isn't enough. Like the Legislature, Government House is making a statement which I can't yet understand. Again I feel an echo . . . not of London this time, but of my own province.

For a start, that cast-iron roof work at the top of the tower . . . it reminds me of the East Block of the Parliament Buildings in Ottawa. But this is a residence . . . and then I have it: Government House could be one of the older mansions in Toronto's Rosedale, or one of those Victorian pillar-of-society homes in a smaller Ontario city such as Cobourg or Brockville. It's a cousin to Sir John A. Macdonald's Teacaddy Castle, remembered from my college days in Kingston. It sits there boldly, like a flagship, almost a miniature of the looming Legislature. Both buildings are rooted in an older culture: again I'm startled to find them here, at the gateway to the West.

By now I know I'm on to something, and so I double back to look at all the statues in the park. Seen from a distance, they're impressively dignified, and redolent of pomp and circumstance. For instance, this first one . . . just up ahead . . . with his arms folded across his chest and a thoughtful look on his face . . . this is surely some great statesman. But, no, it's . . . Robbie Burns! Here in Winnipeg, a statue to the Scottish bard. How curious, I think, as I plunge on to the next one. This is a bust, mounted on a tall plinth, of Sir George Etienne Cartier. It, too, seems misplaced, until I read the inscription which reminds me that the Quebec leader had piloted the bill which brought Manitoba into Confederation. ("May the new province of Manitoba always speak to the inhabitants of the North West the language of Reason, Truth and Justice.") So Cartier certainly has his place in any Manitoban pantheon, but who is this next figure, with the long frock coat, and the noble stance? Why, it's none other then Jon Sigurdsson, "Iceland's Patriot" and (the guide book tells me) a leading man of letters. Curiouser and curiouser. Next I sight a familiar figure, and need no recourse to my book. Seated on a bronze throne, wearing her crown and holding her orb and sceptre, Queen Victoria herself is gazing out imperiously from the steps of the Legislature. (Both monarch and building have the same noble proportions.)

Then I notice a small crowd, clambering about the base of another statue. They're apparently a family, somewhat self-conscious in their Sunday best, and they're posing for the father's camera. When they disperse, I move in closer to discover the identity of the photo's centrepiece. A stolid, seated figure, he has a drooping moustache which reminds me of Lord Kitchener, and a brow which looks like Lenin's. At this point, neither would surprise me, but no . . . this is Taras Schevchenko, "National Poet of the Ukraine, Champion of Justice and Freedom for All."

Just *what* is going on? I'm beseiged by monumental figures, and totally confused by their apparent disparity. Here, for instance, is La Vérendrye, the French explorer and fur trader, and the first white man to reach the confluence of the Red and Assiniboine Rivers. And here is General James Wolfe, who won Canada for Britain, and the Earl of Selkirk, founder of the Red River Settlement, not to mention the Earl of Dufferin, first viceregal visitor to Manitoba after it joined the new Dominion. At the far side of the Legislature, mercifully out of sight of Queen Victoria, I discover a modern, impressionistic statue of Louis Riel, leader of two rebellions against Victoria's crown. (Creighton would have roared to find the traitor here, but I recall that Morton had written of Riel with compassion and restraint.) Finally, I find the Next-of-Kin Memorial, in honour of those who fell in World War One, and a huge totem pole, donated by the native peoples of British Columbia.

Finally, too, even I understood. It was all there: the whole Canadian heritage . . . channeled through Manitoba and still jostling in my mind. French and English and Scottish (I recalled how Burns had stirred the young Morton) . . . native peoples and European minorities . . . the challenge of a new land . . . sacrifice and tribulation (sacrifice for the new territory and, in Europe, for the ancestral lands) . . . allegiance and rebellion . . . commerce and culture . . . com-

munity and diversity . . . the quest for freedom and justice
. . . all of these embodied, not only in the statues, but also in a
Legislature and a Government House which proclaimed in
their confident grandeur that Manitoba was not merely a
wilderness to be exploited, but a testing ground for the best
traditions of European civilization. It was a pageant which
stretched over three centuries and, of course, it was the
essence of Morton's work.

> Harsh is the cackle of the turkey-cocks of Ottawa,
> fighting the while as they feather their mean nests
> of sticks and mud, high on their river bluff. Loud
> sings the Little Man of the Province, crying his
> petty gospel of Provincial Rights, grudging the
> gift of power, till the cry spreads and town hates
> town, and every hamlet of the countryside shouts
> for its share of the plunder and of pelf.

That was Leacock, in 1907, as he decried the failure of
Canadian politicians to rise to the challenge of Canada's
potential. To me, it was an apt description of our public life
in the nineteen-eighties, as Canadians seemed intent on
tearing their country apart in a furor of selfish and short-
sighted bickering. Exploring the grounds of the Legislature,
I had stumbled upon a nobler spectacle: the visual correla-
tive of Leacock's dream and Morton's greatest books. As
much as any of our writers — and certainly more than any
federal or provincial leader — Morton was proclaiming a
sense of nationhood which transcended petty jealousies, and
recalled the aspirations of our nation's founders. It was a
conservative vision which also had, in its concern for minorities and human rights, a strong liberal streak. Walking back
to his apartment, I realized I was confused by this apparent
dichotomy in Morton's thought. How could he be both
conservative and liberal? Surely there had to be some
conflict here. This had to be sorted out; even more, I needed

to discover whether Morton still had faith in his vision, or whether he had succumbed to Creighton's almost apocalyptic pessimism.

It seemed significant that Morton's most hopeful statements about Canada—its moral purpose and its potential for greatness—had been written in the early nineteen-sixties. Like Creighton and other conservative thinkers, he had been appalled by the results of Liberal rule during the two preceding decades: Morton had once condemned Mackenzie King for leading an administration that "rots Canadian life as fungus rots a log". But with the Liberal defeats in 1957 and 1958, Morton proclaimed "a great Conservative resurgence" which offered the opportunity to restore our parliamentary traditions and revive our sense of nationhood. Like the others, though, he soon became aghast at the Conservative performance. By now I was back in Morton's apartment, and asking him to account for this reversal in his hopes. "I never quarrelled with Diefenbaker, but I never trusted him," Morton told me. "He was a radical—not a conservative. He was a personal chauvinist like Trudeau. And he was an incredibly bad leader."

Quebec was another source of disillusionment, along with the general erosion of federal powers. As early as 1964, Morton became alarmed by the drift of the Quiet Revolution, and spoke out against the concept of special status for Quebec. Like Creighton, he warned that such demands flew in the face of history and could lead only to the breakup of Canada. But Morton was much more sympathetic to French Canadian cultural aspirations ("Donald was quite mad on Quebec," he told me), and explicitly supported bilingualism. His Manitoba background had made him open to minority grievances; now he held that the French language should be made official in principle throughout Canada, while leaving it up to the provincial legislatures to decide

when and where it should be practically official. His differences with Creighton led to a public row when Morton wrote
that for English Canada to deny French Canada a full and
free role within Canada was to invoke "cultural continentalism"—the fact that North America spoke English: "This
Professor D. G. Creighton has just done, and distorted by
the act a lifetime of devotion to the understanding of
Canada." (Morton later sprang to the defence of his friend,
however, when Creighton came under attack for his notorious article in *Maclean's*. In a letter to *The Globe and Mail*,
Morton differed with many of Creighton's arguments, but
deplored the "almost hysterical reaction" which they had
received.)

Morton's response to Quebec was based on his conception of a broader Canadian nationality which avoided the
conformist, melting pot pressures of the United States by
giving full scope to cultural and ethnic diversity. In attacking the dominance of English Canada, he stated, French
Canadians were confronting a chimera:

> It no longer matters to any what a man's origin
> is—English, French, German, Ukrainian, Scots,
> Irish, Welsh, Italian—any of all the multitudinous
> strains of Canadian nationality. There is no Brit-
> ish Empire any more: there is no longer any
> adventitious advantage in being English, or dis-
> advantage in not being English. Without any man
> having to turn his back on his past, without any
> fervor of conversion from one nationality to
> another, we have all quietly become Canadians.
> This means that in the future any national major-
> ity will be a varying one, a majority of opinion
> and not of race.

Here again, Morton was speaking with tolerance and
optimism. Yet there were times—especially after the debacle
of the Diefenbaker years—when he seemed to despair of

Canada's survival. In 1964 he wrote that Canada was "so irradiated by the American presence that it sickens and threatens to disolve in cancerous slime." In 1967 he attacked the weakening of the federal government and added that, "I really think the Canadian state is dissolving."

Amid the constitutional convulsions of 1980, however, I found Morton doggedly sanguine about the nation's future. This was no Creighton, roaring out his grief and anger. Instead, in calm and thoughtful sentences, Morton considered the chances that remained to us. In his major books, he had echoed Creighton's dismay over the collapse of Macdonald's concept of Canada; now he seemed resigned to the accumulation of power by the provinces. "We have to accept all that's happened historically," he told me. "We have to create a truly federal system. We have to acknowledge the powers that the provinces *already* have, even if they pretend they don't." True, there was a touch of Creighton—and a flash of sudden passion—when Morton asserted that Quebec separation had to be resisted, if necessary by force. ("We can't sit back and see this country destroyed! To the extent that I despair, I despair of the political innocence of English Canadians.") But Morton was quite ready to envisage an elected Senate with new powers which would give the provinces greater influence within the federal system. And there was an echo of the early Morton when he added with a dry laugh that this reform would have one major benefit: it would end the domination of Parliament by the central provinces.

By now we had been talking for several hours. By now I was no longer discomfited by Morton's reticence. Instead I had an impression of sanity, balance and quiet strength. It was there in the stolidity of Morton's yeoman frame, in his dry, precise voice (with its slight undertone of an English accent) and, of course, in the ideas themselves. There was a quality

about Morton . . . again a word kept trying to emerge and
finally it did . . . *liberal*. Clearly a conservative . . . avowedly a
conservative . . . Morton was also a liberal. Whatever that
meant exactly. For a moment I recalled Leacock's mockery
of all such appellations, at least as they are used in the grab
bag of Canadian politics. (Leacock once described himself as
"Liberal Conservative, or, if you will, a Conservative Liberal
with a strong dash of sympathy for the socialist idea, a friend
of Labour, and a believer in Progressive Racialism. I do not
desire office but would take a seat in the Canadian Senate at
five minute's notice.") Yet there was more to this than party
allegiance, as Morton himself was now quick to confirm.

Characteristically, he began by talking of his family,
and how he came from largely Liberal stock. His paternal
grandfather, the original settler, was a homesteader turned
businessman who was elected to the Manitoba Legislature as
a Liberal. Morton's father also went into politics, first as a
Progressive, and then joined the provincial cabinet as a
Liberal Progressive. On the other side, Morton's maternal
grandfather, another Englishman who probably came out
with the Wolseley expedition, was a lifelong Conservative.
But his daughter, Morton's mother, switched to the Liberals
on her marriage "with an intensity that most Liberals don't
have." (As Morton added laconically: "That was a typical
case of tory loyalty.") Growing up in such a staunchly Grit
household, Morton himself was a nominal Liberal from an
early age; even at Oxford he was barely affected by the
radical politics of the nineteen-thirties, and retained his
Liberal allegiance into early middle age.

Like Creighton, Morton turned to the Conservatives
after World War Two. But the motivation was different.
Through his Manitoban heritage and his studies, Morton was
an adherent to the traditions of British justice; growing up
in a multi-racial community reinforced his commitment to
civil liberties. Although his conversion followed a long
period of intellectual preparation, which included coming

under the influence of Disraeli, the crucial event was the Liberal government's handling of the Gouzenko affair, especially its suspension of basic legal rights for those Canadians suspected of aiding the Soviet Union. Seeking to describe his feelings at the time, Morton wrestled silently with his thoughts. Finally he burst out: "I know it's not fashionable to say this sort of thing—but it was so bloody unBritish! Not in the tradition!"

This excited me: it met head-on a major conflict in my own thinking. Increasingly I was coming to regard myself as a conservative, yet I still clung to certain liberal values. I knew that Canada had evolved as a conservative alternative to the liberal individualism of the United States—an ideology which, in the eyes of the Fathers of Confederation, frequently led to lawless anarchy. While I was glad to be a legatee of their foresight, it was evident that we had swung too often towards the other extreme, and to an extent which dismayed my liberal instincts. Too often, our Canadian imperatives of "peace, order and good government" had been used—by governments of various persuasions—to victimize minorities and stifle independent thought. This was where I always felt at a disadvantage when arguing with socialist and liberal friends: it was too easy for them to blame such excesses on our inherent "conservatism" and timidity, too easy for them to treat me as an enthusiast of the RCMP, if not actually a closet fascist. Now Morton was reminding me that such repressions were *not* in the tradition of British justice—a tradition which went much deeper than the BNA Act or the entire Canadian experience—and that a respect for human rights and human diversity was an essential component of a conservative stance.

Later—and with a similar excitement—I would discover a passage by the American writer Russell Kirk which cast further light on the liberal imperative which lies at the heart of the conservative tradition. Writing of Edmund Burke, the so-called father of modern conservatism, Kirk says:

Liberty, Burke knew, had risen in consequence of an elaborate and delicate process, and its perpetuation depended upon retaining those habits of thought and action which guided the savage in his slow and weary ascent to the state of civil social man. All his life, Burke's chief concern had been for justice and liberty, which must stand or fall together—liberty under law, a definite liberty, the limits of which were determined by prescription. He had defended the liberties of Englishmen against their king, and the liberties of Americans against king and parliament, and the liberties of Hindus against Europeans. He had defended those liberties not because they were innovations, discovered in the Age of Reason, but because they were ancient prerogatives, guaranteed by immemorial usage. *Burke was liberal because he was conservative* [emphasis added].

As with Burke, so with Morton. Moreover, Morton would defend the liberties of suspected Soviet spies because his Manitoban heritage included not only the conservative traditions of British justice, but also such figures as Louis Riel and Taras Schevchenko. When he decided to support the Conservative party, it was in the hope they might prove better than the Grits in protecting our rights. Again, there was more to this than partisan politics, for Morton was evolving a basic philosophical position. This process culminated, in 1959, with his challenging assertion that in the modern era, conservatives were the guardians of true liberalism.

When I first read that statement, it baffled me, and I wondered whether Morton had been visited by Leacock's shade. But Morton's argument was both intricate and serious. Speaking at an academic conference, he outlined the basic principles of conservative thought: respect for authority and respect for tradition, both leading to a firm belief in the need for continuity in human affairs. But continuity did not rule out change. In Canada, there was the dominant tradition of Macdonald: "a conservatism which through responsible government had come to terms with democracy in Canada, and was prepared to move with the times when the need for change was proven." In the twentieth century, conservatism also had to take into account the transformation of agrarian societies into industrial ones, the fantastic results of scientific research, and the enormous acceleration of the pace of social change. Then came the kicker:

> Finally, there is what I would call the end of philosophic individualism, or the extinction of the true liberal. The radical survives, and the socialist, but the liberal who was an individualist, a rationalist, and an internationalist — who was also, be it acknowledged, at his best a humanitarian, and a man of generous instincts and magnanimous mind — that kind of liberal is gone with the top hat and the frock coat. The world is the poorer for his going, and it behoves conservatives to remember that they are in fact his residuary legatees, and that the liberal spirit now finds almost its sole dwelling place in conservative minds.

This was possible — as Morton was now telling me — because conservatism, unlike liberalism or socialism, was not constrained by dogma: "Conservatives are the party of tradition, not the party of ideology. So they can keep going. They can pick up anything, including traditional liberalism. There's no countervailing ideology."

It occurred to me that many a Canadian Liberal might scoff at all this — and especially Morton's contention that the traditional liberal had gone out with the top hat and the frock coat. For it is well known that our Grits present themselves not only as individualists, rationalists and internationalists, but also as generous, magnanimous and humane.

But Morton—again as early as his 1959 speech—would have none of that. For him, the liberal spirit was only rarely to be found in the ranks of the Liberal party. This was because the Grits had become mainly concerned with the growth of state power and technological progress, at the expense of individual freedom. Holding that "people are themselves of absolute value", he called upon conservatives—and the Conservative party—to find ways of protecting individuals from bureaucratic despotism. This did not mean embracing *laissez-faire* economics and rugged individualism, since neither was a conservative principle. Instead, Morton urged the "frank and loyal acceptance of the welfare state, in order to keep it one humanely administered for people, for people who matter as people". He also advocated massive support of the able in education, public patronage of the arts, strengthening the rule of law and the institution of the courts, and reducing the extravagant power of the Prime Minister's office by recreating the tradition of ministerial and parliamentary independence. In these and other ways, Morton concluded, conservatives could best preserve the liberal spirit in Canadian affairs.

This was powerful and provocative. It was also too much to absorb. By now my head was reeling. Neither my mind nor my emotions could take any more. I knew that some sort of breakthrough had been reached—at least in terms of my own quest. When Morton espoused the welfare state, he was not only demolishing all those scarifying stereotypes of the Canadian conservative as arch reactionary. He was also, I realized, approaching the domain of that particular Canadian species, the red tory. This had to be explored in greater detail—and I already had some idea of where to look. For the moment, it was time to rest, and to consider where I'd reached.

I had come to Morton in the hope that his Western conservatism would offer a broader vision of Canada than

Creighton's anglo-tory centralism. This it clearly did—and now there was more. For years, even decades, I had seen myself as some sort of liberal, only to be increasingly dismayed by the results of Liberal rule which, in its arrogance and cynicism, often trod on liberal values. While I was starting to regard myself as a conservative, however, I feared for the hardening of my liberal arteries. Now Morton was showing me that the liberal values which I still cherished could best be preserved through a conservative approach. Indeed, this might well be the *only* way.

As Morton now told me, he was not an instinctive conservative—his Liberal upbringing and liberal inclinations ruled that out. Here he drew a contrast to Creighton: "I'm not known as a conservative in the way that Donald was. But I am a conservative in a way that Donald wasn't." With his help, I managed to resolve the conundrum: Creighton was an instinctive conservative who was never concerned to be a philosophic conservative; Morton, on the other hand, was an instinctive liberal who was converted to conservatism by the process of hard thought.

Later, this came to seem too pat. Reading my notes, and rereading Morton's books and essays, I wondered whether he was more of a natural conservative than he had realized. It was there, I sensed, in his feeling for the land. (This, too, needed more consideration.) And it was there in the very rhythms of his prose, with its echoes of the Anglican Prayer Book and the Athanasian Creed. Morton told me that he had always been a practising Anglican, and that Anglicanism can be important for conservatism: "It gives a sense of establishment, and a sense of social obligation—a sense which makes it possible for a conservative party to be a party of all classes." This was part of Morton's chivalric sense of life—a deep-rooted instinct which also seemed essentially conservative.

There was no doubt, however, that Creighton always gave more of the *appearance* of a conservative in high gear—in other words, a tory. Whatever else, a tory is a Cavalier, which Creighton clearly was. Morton, on the other hand, might be described as a Roundhead's tory. There was something Cromwellian, a touch of the Ironside, to him. If so, this is part of his importance. In a nation which largely adheres to liberal values (even while it often flouts them), a tory like Creighton, with all his passion and flamboyance, is almost an obstacle to the plain man who might otherwise be attracted to conservative thinking. Whereas Morton, with his humane and thoughtful liberalism, can be a *bridge*. Which is what—precisely—he had become for me.

IV

The Particular Landscape:
Al Purdy

Flying back from Winnipeg, I was more than happy with my gleanings. There was a great deal of the conservative tradition which I had yet to explore, but after meeting Morton I knew that much of that tradition was still relevant and might even still be central. Before going any further, however, there was something about Morton which demanded greater grappling, something which might illumine more of the tradition. It was nagging at me as I looked out the aircraft window and watched the tartan of the Manitoba fields give way to the deep blue of Lake Superior, the Group of Seven rockland at the Lakehead and the harsh silhouettes of the grain silos at Thunder Bay. It was, of course, the land itself.

Apart from his liberalism, a strong feeling for the land runs through all of Morton's work. In this he is not unique: the River and the Shield were major protagonists for Creighton.

With Morton, however, the feeling is more direct. Not only in the writing, it was something he conveyed in person. Looking less like a distinguished professor than a prosperous farmer, he had a stolid, rooted quality which embodied his assertion that "the typical Manitoban was a country man, at home with country ways and at ease with the steady rhythm of country life." Morton always wanted something more than this, but something which could be gained without forsaking that basic sense of place. As a farm boy, he had felt an urge to reconcile the actual landscape over which he toiled and the imaginary landscape which his reading was opening in his mind. Literature, history, and philosophy became part of that larger landscape; as he later noted, it was through "passionate thinking" that he was able to bring them all together in his work:

> I think, by way of example, that one fall evening I was rewarded in my search for a landscape in which inner and outer vision were reconciled. It was on a late afternoon flight from Winnipeg to Edmonton one October day. The air was clear except for a vast swirl of smokey cloud across the western horizon in which the sun was dying to glowing ash. The great globe of the prairies rolled majestically below, incised with square stubble and square fallow, engraved by the vast rich valleys, gemmed with lapis lazuli wrought for a Medici, turned by the thumb of old Sebastian Cabot, worked in rough bronze burnished to murky gold, fading off in ridge and coulee into smokey purple or darkening over vast plains in dusky amber—the work either of a Cellini or a Dürer. It was the West of the drifting buffalo herds, of the islanded farmsteads, of Butler, Grove, even of Margaret Laurence. It was my West completely envisioned.

When I first read that passage—with its plangent sense of history—it struck me as a triumphantly conservative vision. After meeting Morton, I began to juggle with the idea that a strong feeling for the landscape—with all its implications—was another distinctive tory trait. It was partly a matter of having reverence for something greater and more enduring than ourselves: it goes without saying that the aircraft which carries Morton high above the prairie is a triumph of modern technology, but it is the vista below which excites the historian's wonder. Partly, too, it was the compulsion to reconcile the inner and outer visions: a conservative needs that sense of deeper unity. There is nothing sentimental about such feelings: time and time again, Morton stressed the harshness of our northern environment, and the dogged heroism which was needed to subdue it. For Morton, this stubborn endurance was part of the "moral purpose" of the Canadian community; his descriptions of the landscape are often lyrical but never bucolic.

True, most Canadians share a similar attitude—whatever their philosophical or political inclinations—since the conquest of a hostile nature is part of our common heritage. In his essay, "In Defence of North America", George Grant argues that our feelings for the land are limited by the fact that our ancestors had to subjugate its harshness and extremities: "That conquering relation to place has left its mark within us. When we go into the Rockies we may have the sense that gods are there. But if so, they cannot manifest themselves to us as ours. They are the gods of another race, and we cannot know them because of what we are, and what we did."

That might be an ultimate truth but there still seemed grounds for distinguishing between liberal and conservative attitudes. With his belief in man's essential freedom, the liberal regards the landscape as something to be subdued and exploited in the name of progress. There is neither reverence nor any sense of roots: nature is something to be used.

To the conservative, on the other hand, man and his world are part of an organic whole—a unity which includes other races, other species and the land itself. His view is always touched with awe: the landscape is important not only for what it can provide, but also for what it has meant to earlier generations, for how it feeds our imaginations, and for the place it holds in some larger natural order of which man is only one component. Grant himself expressed this attitude when he was filmed for a CBC documentary in a rocky cove in Nova Scotia, the home of his forebears. "We live in darkness about important matters, about what nature is, what a person is," he said, as the waves crashed behind him. "We have lost the sense of what lies beyond space and time, beyond our power to manipulate and change. That's why I love this place. It gives me a sense of holiness, of eternity. It reminds me that our traditions, both Greek and Christian, saw the universe as essentially good. The old beliefs recognized limits to man's abilities. They gave us a picture of nature and of man as part of an order, and not a man-made order."

There is much of this sense of wonder in Morton as in Creighton. There is very little similar in the works of such liberal historians as Underhill and Lower. With them, we enter a dry world of wars and treaties, tariffs and debates: man as a measure of all that he encounters. Of course, even conservative historians must deal largely with such practical matters, and it is to our artists that we turn for the most enduring visions of our landscape. The canvases of Tom Thomson and Emily Carr are part of our consciousness; in Canadian literature, as Northrop Frye has noted, everything that is central seems to be marked by the immanence of the natural world. This is not to state that all our artists are tories, and can easily be fitted on some Procrustean bed of conservative conformity. (The membership of the Writers' Union would have collective convulsions at the thought.) But a distinctive tory sensibility has long been at work in our culture. From Haliburton and Mrs. Moodie through Leacock to the present day, it has been especially evident in our literature. There is more to this than a feeling for the land: as Robin Mathews has pointed out, there is a dominant Canadian literary tradition which rejects the typical American individualist hero—such as Huck Finn—and the liberal ideology out of which he springs. Instead, our writers are more often specifically concerned about the choice between the individual and the community: consider, for example, the novels of Sara Jeanette Duncan, Ralph Connor, Frederick Philip Grove, Hugh MacLennan, Adele Wiseman, Robertson Davies, W. O. Mitchell and Margaret Laurence. This, too, seemed essentially conservative—and something to explore. And so I went to see Al Purdy.

AL PURDY! It boggled several minds, that I should want him for this book. "Why, he's the grittiest Grit I know," a fellow poet said. Distinctly bemused, another writer warned that I might not get past the front door. "He's very ethical and helpful to other writers, but he's also gruff. There's something there that wants to bark at you. He's anti-academic and he wears a lower-middle class mask." My friend sighed. "I just can't see you two sitting around the same table."

Suitably cautioned, I nevertheless persevered. For I had been reading a great deal of Purdy, both his poetry and his prose, finding him filled with strong feelings for the land, for roots and ancestors, for the processes of time. I suppose I was finally hooked when I read the Introduction to his collection of magazine articles, *No Other Country*, and found passages like this:

> I take a double view of history, for then and now merge somewhat in my mind. Winnipeg is also Fort Garry and Seven Oaks. Adolphustown, not far from where I live in Prince Edward County, is

the spot where the United Empire Loyalists landed nearly 200 years ago. The restored fortress of Louisbourg in Cape Breton makes me feel like a living ghost, especially when looking at the tombstone of Captain Israel Newton who died there, a member of the colonial army from New England. And driving along the Don Valley Parkway, I think of the old Indian trials that take the same route under black asphalt. In cities everywhere, grass tries to push aside the concrete barriers of the sidewalks.

This had echoes of Morton. On reading it, I knew that Purdy was speaking to the subject of this book. I knew I had to see him. Moreover, my initial letter to Purdy in Ameliasburg received a warm and welcoming response.

I drove down to Prince Edward County on a crisp October morning. The sun was just breaking out as I hit the 401, and the trees were in their full burst of autumn colour. Below Trenton, skirting the Bay of Quinte, it's mostly snakerail fences and old weatherbeaten barns, many with rusted roofs. There are also newish farms, and the modern bungalows of an encroaching suburbia, but the main impression is of a land that's grey and grudging. Purdyland . . . I recognize it from the poems:

> Old fences drift vaguely among the trees
> 　　　　　a pile of moss-covered stones
> gathered for some ghost purpose
> has lost meaning under the meaningless sky
> 　　　　　—they are like cities under water
> and the undulating green waves of time
> 　　　　　are laid on them—

Purdy lives just past the village of Ameliasburg, on the other side of Roblin Lake, down a dead end road. I drive past some ugly bungalows until I spot the home-made A-frame which is mostly old grey barnboard. There's a green outhouse to one side, and also a two-car garage, but the cars themselves are not so much parked as scattered on the untamed grass—two large and venerable gas-guzzlers, one of which seems to be patched together with sticky tape. The front yard is a minor junk heap, littered with piles of wood, wire and plumbing, apparently left over from various building efforts. Gingerly I park amid the debris.

Then Purdy comes out to greet me. A man in his early sixties, he's tall and powerful—six foot three, probably two hundred pounds, with broad shoulders and a deep chest. Bald in front, with stringy, unkempt flaxen hair hanging down from the sides. A wide mouth with thick, sensual lips. A rather large nose and a strong jaw line. He's wearing nondescript brown trousers, a dark blue shirt and a yellow cardigan. And he's chewing on a foul, soggy cigar.

Poets come in all shapes and sizes, and this is certainly no one's stereotype of an aesthete. I remember what my writer friend said: "Someone—I forget who—once described Al as early Greyhound bus station." And I recall the bits and pieces of biography I've put together from newspaper files, his own poems and prose, the anecdotes of other writers, and an excellent monograph by George Bowering. Purdy looks the part... the teenage dropout who rode the rails all the way to B.C. during the Depression... the young man who drove a taxi in Belleville (and bootlegged on the side), as well as working in mattress factories in Vancouver and Montreal... the established poet who used two Canada Council grants to live among the West Coast Indians and the Eskimos of Baffin Island... the restless traveller whose poems bear datelines such as Athens and Havana, Rome and Samarcand, but whose strongest work is often rooted in the land around Ameliasburg... the legendary boozer who's had his scrapes with cops and scraps with women... yes, Purdy looks the part.

Gruff and shy at the same time, Purdy greets me in a friendly way, takes me inside, and sits me down at the kitchen table, behind a plate glass window which looks out on the cool blue lake. On a chair beside me, there's a large green plastic garbage pail full of small red berries and a purple liquid. The smell is pungent, and from time to time the pail gives out an ominous gurgle. "It's my latest batch," Purdy says. "It's only four weeks old — still a ways off." His voice is strong, and booms out when he makes a point. It's a flat Ontario accent, and he often drops the last consonant. Purdy is wearing tinted glasses; I gradually notice that his eyes are shrewd and he's watching my reactions closely.

For the first hour or so, it's mostly sparring, as we feel each other out. Purdy makes us coffee, and a lunch of eggs and sausages. (Eurithe, his wife of forty years, is visiting a sister in Vancouver.) Awkward and apprehensive, I would have welcomed a stiff drink to loosen my tongue. Still, I start to talk about my book, mentioning Creighton and Morton, and somehow stumbling on to the monarchy. "The monarchy puts me off," Purdy says firmly. All right, I concede, but surely our British parliamentary traditions ... "I'm not keen on them, either," Purdy breaks in. "I don't see any particular virtue in them. Any democracy can work out its own system, and have its own head of state."

By now I'm floundering, and beginning to wonder whether I'm wasting our time, but finally I lurch on to some common ground. Back in the late sixties, Purdy edited a book called *The New Romans* in which some forty Canadian writers expressed their strong aversion to American domination. (In his Introduction, Purdy concluded that it might already be too late to retrieve our sovereignty: "Therefore, all this book may do is register a sullen protest, a belated yap from a captive dog.") I tell him how much it meant to me then, how I'm still tired of Liberal pussy-footing, how I'm basically anti-American. "I'm anti-American, too," Purdy says. "There's a lot to admire in the United States, but I hate the American arrogance, especially when it's directed at us."

Then he tells me about a turning point—a trip he made to Havana in 1964 as a guest of the Castro government and at the instigation of a Canadian committee called Fair Play for Cuba. There were eleven others in the group, including Pierre Trudeau. At one point, they were sitting at little desks in a school house, listening to an official explain that Cuba was a very democratic place. Purdy put his hand up and asked about free elections. Trudeau leaned forward and said in a very audible whisper: "Don't be naive, Al." Purdy tells it with a laugh. Although his poems from the trip show that he was anything but naive about the nature of the Castro regime, Purdy was stirred by the sheer excitement of the Cuban revolution. ("Everyone joins hands and sings together / a million voices and bodies / sway back and forth in the sunlight"). As he tells me now: "They were free of the United States and they were exulting in it. It was all very exhilarating. My nationalism grew from there."

Now I recall how my own nationalism grew out of my trips to Vietnam, during the period of heaviest American intervention. I saw what the Americans were actually doing to the fabric of Vietnamese society, and I came to be disgusted by the complicity of their Canadian surrogates, who were allegedly involved in peace-keeping and peace-making, but who were actually more concerned to further the cause of the American imperialists. This attitude implied no admiration for the Vietnamese communists, nor was it inconsistent with a tory philosophy. As Morton wrote, conservatism is always potentially revolutionary because it rests on organic change: "To the conservative natural growth is the essence of being."

Now, too, we're off and running. No longer sparring, for the next four or five hours we're deep in Purdy's odyssey and his feelings for Canada. When Purdy talks about his nationalism, he's anything but bombastic. "I detest the American kind of nationalism because it's imperialistic and imposes itself on other nations. I don't like the word 'love'

used about a country—it's sticky." Instead he talks in terms
of land and family—with a concreteness and a lack of
Victorian sentimentality which also echoes Morton. As he
now tells it, when he came back from Cuba as a newly
awakened nationalist, he was prompted into deeper exploration of his own roots, and the particular history of Prince
Edward County.

Of English, Irish and Scottish stock, Purdy had grown
up in nearby Trenton, the son of a farmer who died when Al
was two. It was a lower-middle class background; while both
parents descended from Loyalists, nothing much was made of
this around the home. Nor did he have much early enthusiasm for Trenton. ("A grave pall of depression still settles
over me when I approach that town.") When he and Eurithe
returned to the region in 1957, it was strictly out of desperation. His poetry had still to win him public acclaim, and he
had been working in a Montreal mattress factory while
writing plays for the CBC on the side. But few of the plays
were sold, and in his early forties Purdy concluded that he
was a failure. With $1,000 of unemployment insurance, he
and Eurithe moved to Ameliasburg and started to construct
the A-frame with a pile of used lumber bought in Belleville.
"I said I'd never work again in any job. We quarrelled
violently over how to build the place. All the neighbours
pitied my wife for having such a no-good husband."

The neighbours thought that Purdy was crazy, and his
wife even crazier to stay with him. With no electricity or
plumbing in the A-frame, the winters were especially cruel.
For water, Purdy had to chop through three or four feet of
lake ice. An iron cook stove was the only source of heat: it
kept Purdy busy hacking at old railway ties and some of the
left-over lumber. Despite his sense of failure, Purdy never
stopped writing. Even before the trip to Cuba, he was
checking out the village, talking to old-timers, searching for
material. Wandering the roads, he began looking at old
farmhouses—not as an expert, but with the idea that they

expressed the characters of their builders. Although he would set his poems in many other parts of Canada—and several other countries—he was starting to find the heart of his poetic world in the farms and villages of southeastern Ontario, with a growing sense that the landscape, the buildings and the people were all linked in some endless process of change and continuity:

> and if I must commit myself to love
> for any one thing
> it will be here in the red glow
> where failed farms sink back into the earth
> the clearings join and fences no longer divide
> where the running animals gather their bodies together
> and pour themselves upward
> into the tips of falling leaves
> with mindless faith that presumes a future

That first year in Ameliasburg, Purdy began to explore the ruin of an old grist mill. It was four storeys high, with grey stone walls that were three feet thick. Purdy marvelled at the 24-inch wide boards, from giant pines chopped down more than a century earlier, and at the hand-carved cogs and gears. More than that, he began to wonder about the men who had built and used the mill—the pioneers, most of them Loyalists, who had made their homes in the wilderness because they had no other place to go. In particular he asked old-timers about Owen Roblin, who put up the mill in 1842, who lived to be 97, and who is buried in the Ameliasburg graveyard. (He is also an ancestor of Duff Roblin, the former Conservative premier of Manitoba.) This was the starting point for many of Purdy's Roblin Lake poems, and notably for the book-long work, *In Search of Owen Roblin*:

> In the midst of my own despair and failure
> I wrote it all down on paper
> everything I learned about Roblin's Mills

and the 19th-century village now called Ameliasburg
in a kind of fervid elation at knowing
the privilege of finding a small opening
in the past, shouting questions and hearing echoes
whispering in the tents of the living

Through this opening in the past, Purdy recreates not
only Owen Roblin, but also other settlers of the region,
including his own grandfather, Ridley Neville Purdy, whom
he could just remember from his boyhood. Without false
sentiment, he pictures them as giants, marvelling at their
fortitude and courage. In 1858, at age 18, his grandfather set
out for the lumber camps, in search of his first job:

his face the fresh ruddy face of a farm boy
smeared with grease to protect himself
against wild black flies and blazing sun
sweating dust on a road leading into the sky
with a single black cloud near the horizon
a red kerchief wrapped around his head
biscuits and dried deer meat for lunch
six feet tall but only 200 pounds then
axe balanced on his shoulders and stepping it out
the lifelong journey to anywhere
having decided to live forever
between these blue folded hills
of the hawk's surveillance and the sun's dominion

To Purdy, these Loyalists are not heroes in any conventional sense. In old age, his grandfather is "250 slagheap
pounds of ex-lumberjack / barnbuilder and backwoods
farmer / all-night boozer and shanty wrestler / prime example of a misspent life / among ladies of the church sewing
circle / poker player and teller of tall tales". In the midst of
his despair, however, Purdy draws strength from the human
links which bind him to his past, and to the landscape which
he inhabits and over which his ancestors toiled:

In search of Owen Roblin
I discovered a whole era
that was really a backward extension of myself
built lines of communication across two centuries
recovered my own past my own people
a long misty chain stretched thru time
of which I am the last but not final link

. . . . .

The black millpond
                holds them
movings and reachings and fragments
the gear and tackle of living
under the water eye
all things laid aside
                  discarded
                    forgotten
but they had their being once
and left a place to stand on

It was Edmund Burke who saw the state as a partnership not just among the living, but among those who are living, those who are dead, and those who are yet to be born. This was at the core of Burke's philosophy, and it is essential to any conservative vision. A similar feeling for human continuity is strong in Purdy. As David Helwig has written: "If there is one theme that is central in Purdy, it is the sense of the mystery of time by which things happen and are lost, happen and endure."

Although this theme is at the heart of the Roblin Lake poems, it stretches far beyond Loyalist Ontario in much of Purdy's other work. Land, animals, people—all are seen as part of the continuum, and nothing is ever finally lost. In his "Lament for the Dorsets" (Eskimos who became extinct in the fourteenth century), Purdy imagines the last of the tribe working on an ivory carving: "the carving is laid aside / in beginning darkness / at the end of hunger / and after a while wind / blows down the tent and snow / begins to cover him / After 600 years / the ivory thought / is still warm". At other times, Purdy feels a link not only with long-dead ancestors and extinct Eskimos, but also with some of the most ancient creatures. On the Galapagos Islands, he scratches the neck of a 160-year-old tortoise (whom he names Moses) and remembers " . . . far ages / when birds and mammals / branched off from reptiles / and therefore those distant / ancestors of old Moses / are unrecognizable / but yet indubitably / my own".

And, always, Purdy returns to his sense of the land. As George Woodcock has noted: "Al Purdy's writing fits Canada like a glove; you can feel the fingers of the land working through his poems." More than this, Purdy has a conservative feeling for the land as something greater and more enduring than ourselves, something held in trust, not merely something to be exploited. In "A Handful of Earth"—an ostensibly political poem addressed to René Lévesque—he writes that the *fleur-de-lis* and the maple leaf are only symbols, and that our true language speaks from inside the land itself: "I wondered who owns this land / and knew that no one does / for we are tenants only".

Back at the A-frame, we're discussing all this, but in fits and starts, without much coherence. Purdy isn't being difficult or evasive—just the opposite—but he rambles a lot, and it's hard to keep him on one track. Which is not too surprising—when he invited me down, Purdy wrote that he wasn't sure my book would benefit from my talking to him: "Feelings are pretty intangible, and so are visions. Perhaps they come out better as poems than prose." So it's fitting that he shows me the galley proofs of his latest collection, to be

published as *The Stone Bird*. He picks out three or four for
me to read. In the one I like best, "The Darkness", Purdy
recalls chasing a porcupine out of his house, and feeling
affection for it, as if it embodied all the lost, doomed animals
crushed to death on highways or eaten by fiercer animals;
then he's looking into the night-time sky and wondering at
his own insignificance ... well, it *doesn't* come out well as
prose, but there is one passage near the end which moves me
and intrigues me:

> What this comes to is religion
> not the conventional stuff
> but some lost kind of coherence
> I've never found in people
> or in myself for that matter
> only in the unhurried natural world
> where things are uncrowded by things
> with distance between animals
> star distance between neighbours
> when the grouchy irritable universe
> fumbles with understanding
> and a god's coherence
>   Look down on me
> spirit of everyplace
> guardian beyond the edge of chaos
> I may be a slight reminder
> of a small tribe that occurred to you
> when you were thinking of something else
> even tho I am of little importance
> and conversely of great importance

Warily, I say this seems quite reverential. Purdy doesn't
quibble, and goes on to state that he finds his new work more
contemplative and less exuberant than his earlier poems.
Then he's off on another tack, but later it occurs to me that,
yes, it's almost inevitable that he should have written something like that passage. If you muse long enough on change

and continuity, on your links to the land and long-dead ancestors, you have to be concerned with coherence, and finally you're led to acknowledge some greater force, some larger order that man's philosophy cannot plumb or fathom, and that man's poetry can only touch upon with awe. "There is an order that keeps things fast in their place," said Burke, again reaching to the core of the conservative vision; "it is made to us, and we are made to it."

But this is no time to bring up Burke. By now we are into the wine, and our conversation is even more rambling than before. At first Purdy apologizes for not having any beer. ("I always basically mistrust anyone who doesn't drink beer," he once wrote. "They generally turn out to be stuffed shirts.") Then he thought he'd just taste the wine to see how it was, sinking a cup in the soggy mash. "A bit dry," he says. "Some would say sour. Perhaps it's stayed there long enough." I try a glass. It *is* sour, and also rough and tangy. But drinkable, just drinkable. "Are you feeling better now?" Purdy asks me, several glasses later, in a shrewd, sly way.

After a while we need to clear our heads and bladders, so we wander outdoors. Purdy takes me into a nearby shed which holds his workroom. At first it's hard to see anything through the cigar smoke—a permanent fug. Gradually I make out a great clutter of papers on an old metal desk (Purdy says it cost him $50) which also has an ancient Royal typewriter ($25). There are eight or so empty bottles—gin, whisky and wine—scattered on the floor. Gradually, too, I notice that the walls are lined with books—a remarkable collection of Canadiana. "I know more about Canadian books than any other Canadian writer," Purdy says. (It's the only boast he makes all day.) Then he shows me some of his treasures. A rare edition of Bartlett sketches opens at a crested bookplate. "This belonged to some earl or other," Purdy says, and it strikes me that the dismissive tone is quite deliberate. Next there's a copy of Samuel Hearne's *Journey from the Prince of Wales Fort in Hudson's Bay to the Northern*

Ocean, an edition of George Heriot's *Travels Through the Canadas* and others which I don't know but which are clearly old and splendid. There is also a large volume called *Canadian Wild Flowers* with several striking colour plates. As Purdy carefully turns the pages, I notice his hands. They're big and strong, the fingers flair out to the tips, and the nails are well manicured, as though Purdy takes a pride in them. As he goes on to show me other books, it's clear he has a love of fine printing and binding, a sensuous feeling for the touch and texture of a book.

Then there's a local history of Prince Edward County by Richard and Janet Lunn which mentions one "Purdy the sweet singer of Ameliasburg"—a man who went around the settlements in the early nineteenth century, singing for his living. "It puts me off," Purdy says, and then mumbles something about not wanting to seem "a long-haired poet". Next he shows me another large volume called *Pioneer Life in the Bay of Quinte*, with genealogies of old families, including several called Purdy. There's a McDagg Purdy and a lot of Wellington Purdys, among others. "I guess they're my people," Purdy says, diffidently. "Wellingon is my own middle name—it's always embarrassed me." Yet I suspect he's much prouder than he chooses to let on. "I'm not an ancestor worshipper." he says firmly, but then adds quickly: "One has ambiguous feelings about everything."

Yes, there is an ambiguity. Most of the time, Purdy appears in the guise of a tough guy—the beer-swilling, aggressively ramshackle slob who disdains academics and aesthetes and who delights in flouting civilized conventions. "My idea of privacy," he told me, minutes after I'd arrived, "is that you can take a piss in your own front yard." (We did.) Stating that he could never read Proust, he burst out: "My God, they're long-winded bastards—all the great authors!" (Later, though, he urged me to read *One Hundred Years of Solitude*, that massive masterpiece by Gabriel Garcia Marquez, calling it one of the great books of the century.) When I introduced Jung into the conversation, he stumbled over the pronunciation, and again it seemed deliberate. "I can never get all those funny European names," he added truculently. Some months later, when I went to hear Purdy read from his new book at Toronto's Harbourfront, he was again playing the part of a belligerent churl, appearing in a garish red-checked shirt, shambling to the microphone and chomping on another of his foul cigars ... as if to tell the audience: "If you've got some high-falutin' notion of a poet ... well, just take a look at *me!*" After reading from "The Darkness", with that fine reverential passage, he looked down sardonically from the podium: "Pretty philosophical, eh?"

Yet this is also the man who cares deeply about his roots and traditions, who takes a pride in fine books which is both scholarly and sensuous, who is remarkably well read, and who fills his poems—however colloquial their style—with frequent classical allusions, following some homely passage with a reference to Sappho or Tamerlaine. According to George Bowering, this last is a deliberate tactic: Purdy gains strength from being neither exclusively primitive nor exclusively academic, and so keeps the literati off their guard. To Bowering, it is also part of Purdy the Canadian: "Canadians are taught to disguise their learning and their sensitivity in order not to appear pushy or pretentious ... "

That seemed very true—not only of Purdy, but also of myself and many others. For most of this century, Canada has seen the triumph of the liberal levellers, secular Calvinists who despise anyone or anything which has claims to quality and finer feeling. Jealous and spiteful, they would cut everyone and everything down to their own level of insipid mediocrity. To survive in such a grudging milieu, those who strive for excellence often feel the need to mask their real intentions. Learned early, the impulse soon becomes instinctive.

So, it would seem, with Purdy. Behind that mask of barnyard grit, there lurks a conservative sensibility. It is a sensibility quite different from those of Creighton and Morton since there is little philosophical about it, and nothing specifically political. ("I'm a sort of hazy socialist," Purdy told me. "An NDP type.") But the poet who sees everything—land, ancestors, himself, creatures yet unborn —as part of some unending process, some larger order, some lost kind of coherence . . . that man is a conservative.

By now I knew that tories came in many guises. If I was starting to sense some underlying unity, I was even more struck by the diversity of temperaments. If Creighton was a conservative tory, and Morton a liberal conservative, then Purdy was a folk tory—as such, he had shown me another major strand in the tradition.

Perhaps Leacock was right to mock at all such labels. But I was starting to think that tories *had* to come in many guises, as a function of their lack of ideology, and even as a prerequisite for survival in a liberal era. At any rate, I knew there was more to come. And so, with another anxious glance in the direction of Leacock, I decided to confront one of his old colleagues, a man who seemed to be that strangest of all conservative hybrids, the socialist tory.

V

Red Tories and Social Justice:

Eugene Forsey

Pacing up and down his Senate office, Eugene Forsey was delivering a barrage of epigrams and anecdotes. Suddenly he stopped in mid-sentence, sprang almost to attention, and recited a favorite credo: "I'm an unrevised, unrepented Sir John A. Macdonald conservative . . . " Forsey paused for effect. "There aren't many of us left . . . " Another pause. "Just Creighton and me . . . " Yet another pause. "That is . . . if Donald will admit me to the sacred precincts!" Now the eyes were twinkling and Forsey was almost laughing. Then—just as abruptly—he was speaking with real anger: "I'm sick of listening to pygmies trying to destroy what giants created!"

This was during my first meeting with Forsey. It was at a time when Ottawa and the provinces were battling over Pierre Trudeau's plan to patriate the constitution. Forsey was in the thick of the fray, busily defending Macdonald's concept of strong central government against those whom he scornfully called "the province-worshippers".

By now, Forsey had been talking for nearly two hours. Although in his mid-seventies, he was showing no sign of strain. Somewhat on the short side, somewhat stooped, he was also brisk and emphatic, both in speech and movement. A perky, dapper man in a deep blue suit. With his abundant grey moustache, he was almost debonair, reminding me of Adolphe Menjou. Forsey has a high-pitched voice with a Newfie/Irish lilt which serves as an impeccable instrument for his anecdotes, running a gamut of accents and emotions, seldom faltering amid the torrent of perfectly crafted stories. He was totally in command. I vaguely remembered— somewhere at the start of the interview—asking him to discuss his roots. Since then I managed to interject only an occasional word, trying with mimimal success to direct the flow of reminiscence. "I'm in my anecdotage," he said at one point, and it came out proudly. Renowned for his memory, and for his mimicry, Forsey was giving me Sir Wilfred Laurier addressing an election meeting from the back of a railway car, as well a ponderous Sir Robert Borden and a peevish Mackenzie King, not to mention Stephen Leacock and a host of lesser academics. There was one story from the nineteen-thirties—it lasted for fifteen minutes—which involved six or seven McGill professors of distinctive racial origins: Forsey took all the parts, and managed all the accents.

In this—if little else—he reminded me of John Diefenbaker. Shortly before his death, the Chief had regaled me with a cast of characters ranging from Churchill and de Gaulle through a multitude of eccentric judges, small town drunks and long-forgotten political hacks. Merciless in his imitations, Dief would suddenly weep—to illustrate how Harold MacMillan had tried to win negotiating points— or stand to mime Jack Pickersgill's distinctive waddle. Forsey was the same, revelling in his showmanship. Unlike Diefenbaker, however, Forsey has humility. When I first wrote to request a meeting, he replied:

I need hardly say I should be highly honoured to figure in such distinguished company in your new book, though I fear George Grant looks upon me with a very jaundiced eye, and might jib at finding himself in such *bad* company. I am, however, very doubtful about whether you ought to bother with me, at any rate in anything more than perhaps a few footnotes. Leacock, Creighton and Grant are towering figures; I am simply not in the same class.

For all his modesty, Forsey had a special fascination. Almost single-handed, he seemed to demolish most conventional concepts of "left" and "right". For a start, there was no doubt about his socialist credentials. As a young academic, Forsey helped to draft the Regina Manifesto which led to the formation of the CCF. Through the Depression and World War Two, he peppered the pages of the *Canadian Forum* with his incisive left-wing polemics. For more than two decades, Forsey worked at the heart of the trade union movement as research director for the Canadian Labour Congress. In his old age, he was still quick to fulminate in print against the attempts of "neo-conservatives" to undermine Canada's heritage of public enterprise.

But there is another side to Forsey which is perhaps even more familiar to the public, especially those who watch the television news. Our greatest constitutional expert, he has been as vehement as Creighton in his defence of our British parliamentary traditions and Macdonald's vision of Confederation. In fact, it was Creighton who suggested that Forsey should have a place in this book, or, indeed, in any book about Canadian tories. Creighton had written an admiring introduction to Forsey's collected essays, *Freedom and Order* (itself a very tory title), and the book is dedicated to Arthur Meighen, the former Conservative leader who was Forsey's greatest personal and political hero.

To add to the confusion, there is Forsey's record of shifting partisan allegiance. In the nineteen-forties, he contested four elections for the CCF (and lost each time). Later he broke with his party's successor, the NDP, and supported Diefenbaker and the Conservatives. Later still he backed Trudeau with effusive praise, and was appointed to the Senate as a Liberal. Then, in 1982, he quit the Liberal party, citing the government's reaction to the McDonald Commission on RCMP wrongdoing, and its arbitrary cuts in railway passenger services, and complaining that it suffered from "an imperfect understanding of the rule of law".

Few opponents ever suggested that Forsey acted through expediency, or lack of principle. But how did he reconcile those principles — this tory who is also a socialist, and for many years a Liberal? Perhaps it could happen only in Canada. (Again, I thought I heard a distinctive Leacockian chuckle.) At any rate, it seemed best to start at the beginning.

When I asked Forsey about his roots, he responded with alacrity. Suddenly we were back in the eighteenth century, and he was reeling off names and origins of a host of ancestors, much faster than I could write them down. According to legend, one of the ancestors was the pilot who guided Wolfe's fleet up the river to Quebec; at any rate, both branches of the family were settled in British North America by 1800. His father's people came from Devon to Newfoundland; on his mother's side there were Irish Protestants, as well as Loyalists and pre-Loyalists of English and Dutch stock, who moved to Nova Scotia from New York and Massachusetts. As Forsey writes in his preface to *Freedom and Order*: "A belief in, and a devotion to, British institutions, was certainly bred in my bones; and in the home in which I was brought up, politics, especially Canadian politics, was meat and drink."

That home was in Ottawa, where Forsey grew up under the powerful influence of his maternal grandfather, William Clark Bowles. He had come there with his mother in 1904, when he was six months old, after the death of his father. His grandfather had been a page in the Assembly of Canada at the age of eleven; by the time he took over the care of his grandson, William Bowles was the long-time Chief Clerk of the House of Commons and (according to Forsey) just about the best informed Canadian on parliamentary procedure. "I remember the debate on the Naval Bill very well," Forsey recalled. "My grandfather worked all night for two solid weeks. It made a great impression on me." That was in 1912, when Forsey was eight. Before long, politics were his passion, even his recreation. While other boys played hockey and football, he haunted the galleries of the House of Commons, absorbed in both the ritual and the substance of the great debates. It must have been a strange childhood. A contemporary at the Ottawa Normal School recalls that Forsey was always accompanied by his mother: "He was invariably dressed in what we felt was sissy attire—bare knees, sailor blouses or shirts with Eton collars, and always a big floppy bow tie. That—and his squeaky voice—did nothing to endear him to the rest of us. But for his mother's militantly protective presence, I'm sure he would have had a very bad time."

Inside the home, the political atmosphere was strongly conservative. "My grandfather had to be non-partisan in the House, but he was a devoted follower of Sir John A. He was very proud that Macdonald once told him: 'Willie, Willie, you're indispensable to me.'" (This, of course, in broad Scots.) But if the early influences were conservative, it is tempting to find a source of Forsey's later radicalism in the prevailing family religion. His father was a Methodist probationer who strained his heart by working himself to exhaustion in the remote Newfoundland mission fields. "He'd go out in all kinds of weather, and gave away his warm clothes to the poor." Eventually his father went to Mexico for his health and, still over-working, died there. (This, Forsey said, explained his mother's protectiveness. "Every time I sneezed she told people I was prone to bronchitis, just like my father. In fact, I've never had a chest cold in my life.") In Ottawa, the family attended Dominion Methodist Church, which had a comfortable, middle-class congregation. As such, it was hardly a breeding ground for the Social Gospel which was leading Methodists like Salem Brand and J. S. Woodsworth into socialist politics: according to Forsey, little was heard of their ideas in Ottawa when he was growing up. In later years, however, Forsey's sense of Christian duty served to feed his indignation at the injustices in Canadian life. In 1934, as a charter member of the Fellowship for a Christian Social Order, he signed this statement of purpose: "Believing as we do that there are no distinctions of power and privilege in the Kingdom of God, we pledge ourselves in the serivce of God and to the task of building a new society in which all exploitation of man by man and all barriers to the abundant life which are created by the private ownership of property shall be done away." When Forsey was converted to socialism, his Methodism was certainly no hindrance.

This conversion began at McGill, where Forsey took economics and political science. At first his home-grown conservatism was reinforced by Leacock, the head of the department, whom Forsey recalls as a masterful teacher. ("He could have done absolutely anything. He could have been Prime Minister.") Then there was the equally powerful example of Meighen, whom Forsey had often heard in the House of Commons, speaking in flawless sentences for two or three hours at a stretch, without a single note. ("He was far and away the most brilliant parliamentarian this country has ever produced.") Soon, however, Forsey was being swayed by Leacock's deputy, Joe Hemmeon, who called himself a Communist, and by the minister of Forsey's church, an English Wesleyan in the radical tradition. Forsey began to consider himself a socialist in 1926. As he recalled it, the turning point came when the old guard Conservatives began conspiring to remove Meighen from the leadership. "The business establishment, especially in Montreal, thought that Meighen was a dangerous radical. When I wrote an article for the student newspaper, defending Meighen as a progressive, I was called on the carpet by the principal, Sir Arthur Currie. He spent one whole hour accusing me of 'Bolshevism'. Imagine that—I was a Bolshevik because I supported the leader of the Conservative party!"

When a Rhodes Scholarship took Forsey to Balliol in 1926, he lost little time in joining the Oxford Labour Club. It would be several years before the Depression made social-ism a respectable cause for undergraduates; at the time, Oxford was more notable for the modish dilettantes whom Evelyn Waugh was starting to satirize. There was nothing so flippant about Forsey. On the boat to England, he caught the attention of another young Canadian, the future diplomat Charles Ritchie. "I got into conversation with a graduate student, also on his way to Oxford." Ritchie wrote in his diary. "He is a fine intelligent young man called Forsey. He has read all the serious articles in political science magazines and attended sessions in the House of Commons in Ottawa and taken notes of the proceedings. He will probably be a figure in Canadian public life. Why can't I be more like him?"

Half a century later I would be struck by other qualities in Forsey, in particular his impish wit and suppressed mirth. If these came to modify his severity, it seems that Forsey has always been something of a puritan. ("You can't imagine Eugene doing anything radically indecent," George Grant told me, and then roared with laughter.) "I come off pretty well as regards the sins of the flesh." Forsey said after I encouraged him to assess his achievements. "I don't drink and I wouldn't know a prostitute if I tripped over one." That prompted him to recall a visit he made to Berlin, during his time at Oxford, along with King Gordon, another future stalwart of the Canadian left. In the dying days of the

Weimar Republic, the capital was notorious for its deca-
dence. "An American foreign correspondent challenged us to
walk down 'the most sinful block in the world.' He said it was
impossible not to be accosted, impossible not to succumb.
Well, we walked down it. Nobody looked at us."

Back in Canada in 1929, Forsey began a twelve-year stint as a
sessional lecturer in his old department at McGill. As he
recalls the period, he was always in trouble for his socialist
views. ("I was a constant headache to the authorities.")
Although the quarrel was later patched up, Leacock was
aghast at his star pupil's apostasy. ("He told Hemmeon he
wanted to shoot me.") Regarded with suspicion by Sir
Arthur Currie and other members of the university establishment, Forsey never received a promotion and never
achieved tenure. When he finally sought an explanation
from the Dean, he was told that he was 'injudicious'. Pressed
for an example, the Dean replied: "You have been heard in
this building speaking in an excited tone of voice."

Telling the story, Forsey mimicked the Dean's prissy
voice. Then he snorted with indignation. But he was also
enjoying himself enormously, and was soon embarked on a
whole string of anecdotes, each of them involving a confrontation with authority. By now I was starting to suspect that a
passion for disreputation was a trait among Canadian tories:
certainly they relished their rows. Early on in my research I
had made this note to myself: "Explore *anger* as a component
of the conservative mentality . . . relate this to my general
sense of anger throughout the land . . . its basis: the failure of
the liberal North American Dream." At that point I wasn't
prepared to make the larger connection, but I was accumu-
lating evidence that the Canadian tory was often a notable
curmudgeon.

This was true of Leacock, despite the popular image (as
in the famous Karsh photograph) of a genial humorist,
everyone's favourite uncle. Leacock *was* benevolent, and

avuncular. (When I visited one of his oldest surviving friends, John Drinkwater, then 95, in an Orillia hospital, the first thing he recalled was Leacock's drinking and his profanity. The second was his kindness: he dwelt on this.) In his writing, although the satire often bites, there is seldom any malice. But Leacock was also a man of strong passions: he had a quick temper and was loth to forgive his enemies. As an early example, there was the banishing of his father, a wandering drunkard and habitual failure. In 1887, when Stephen was seventeen, Peter Leacock went away for the last time, possibly after an incident with a carving knife. Stephen drove the cutter to the station. White-faced and brandishing the buggy whip, he told his father: "If you ever come back, I'll kill you!" (Peter took the hint. Although a failure, he was also a survivor, eventually changing his name to Captain Lewis, taking a common-law wife and settling in Nova Scotia, where he died at the age of 92, only three years before his famous son. Unlike other family members, Stephen always refused to visit him.)

Creighton, of course, seemed perpetually angry, and was notorious for his disputes. His close friend and publisher, John Gray, called him The Terrible-Tempered Mr. Bang, after a comic strip character. Aside from lashing out at Mackenzie King and other Liberals in his writings, Creighton also conducted running feuds with several fellow professors, most notably Frank Underhill, his colleague at the University of Toronto and a leading continentalist. According to Robert Fulford, Underhill said he finally left the university because he couldn't stand any more Creighton. Nor were Creighton's friends and ideological allies immune from his wrath: his views on Quebec provoked public disputes with Morton and George Grant. "I've had a few Homeric rows," Creighton told me. He went on to describe a younger historian as very venomous. "I suppose I'm venomous, too," he added.

Among his other quarrels, Forsey recalled a chance encounter with Grant in the corridors of McMaster Univer-

sity. "I greeted him in a friendly way, but he glared at me
furiously and denounced me to my face. He called me the
most docile Liberal in the Senate!" (Forsey added that Grant
made a handsome apology, and Grant later told me he was
thoroughly ashamed of his rudeness: "It was his obsequious-
ness to Trudeau . . . Trudeau is a slicky.") Later, too, I would
find that Grant's own conversation was spiked with frequent
barbs at the expense of Vincent Massey (his uncle), Lester
Pearson and a host of other prominent Canadians.

There seemed no end to it, and it appeared that tories
had an innate complusion not only to savage their enemies,
but also to swipe at each other. True, there was little of the
curmudgeon to William Morton. Yet in discussing his move
to Trent University from Manitoba, Morton said in passing:
"There was a bust-up. I had a row with the President." And
he agreed with me that asperity, passion and quarrelsome-
ness *were* common to a lot of conservatives. (He added a few
more examples, most notably Diefenbaker.) "It's hard to
generalize," Morton went on, "but strong individuality is a
tory trait. The lack of ideology means you're on your own.
And, I suppose, it's also a matter of tories having more
heart."

Not only more heart, but also stronger principles. Later
it would occur to me that anger, spleen and satire are the
logical outcome when a conservative with his belief in a
larger moral and political order confronts a world which is
manifestly flawed. With his suspicion and spite, Dean Swift
is a classic example. As Nigel Dennis has written, these were
the products not of meanness, but of frustrated idealism:

> If we refuse to accept Swift as an idealist of dignity
> and a man of rigid, passionate principles, we cannot
> hope to understand why he is driven so easily by
> any betrayal of these into the most scabrous rages
> and revengeful emotions. His wiser friends under-
> stood this very well, and refused flatly to credit the
> misanthropy and disdain of the human race that

we, today, believe to have been true of Swift. "If
you despised the world as much as you pretend."
Bolingbroke tells him coolly, "you would not be so
angry with it."

Back in Ottawa, Forsey was recalling his most famous
row—one which emphasized his conservatism, rather than
his socialism. He started the story while sitting at his desk,
under a portrait of the Queen. Soon he began to swivel in his
chair, throwing out his arms and slapping his thighs to
emphasize a point, Finally his passion brought him to his
feet—by the end, he was again pacing up and down the
room.
 The controversy had begun with an event which seemed
destined to interest only a handful of academics, In 1943,
Forsey published a book which was based on his long years
of constitutional studies, *The Royal Power of Dissolution of
Parliament in the British Commonwealth*. This was a detailed
survey of the precedents of grant and refusal of dissolution;
in examining the Canadian constitutional crisis of 1926 (the
"King-Byng affair"), it firmly supported the Governor-
General against the Liberal Prime Minister, and accused
the latter of running roughshod over the rights of parliament. This was anathema to John Dafoe, the powerful editor
of the *Winnipeg Free Press*, a staunch liberal who hated tories,
socialists and anything that smacked of "British imperialism". As Creighton wrote: "Dafoe had been one of the chief
prophets and expositors of the Grit-Liberal interpretation of
Canadian history, and he realized instinctively that this
divine revelation was threatened by the impious heresy of
Eugene's book." After Dafoe attacked the book in two
successive issues of the *Free Press*—devoting seven columns
to the task—Forsey replied in a letter that the review was
"compounded of about equal parts of misrepresentation and
abuse." When he printed the letter, Dafoe added a brief note
accusing Forsey of having evaded his chief criticism.

Forsey was going to let the matter rest, but he was urged to retaliate by both the conservative Arthur Meighen and the socialist T. C. Douglas. ("In almost identical words, they told me to let him have it with both barrels.") The ensuing exchange lasted three months and aroused wide interest, with B. K. Sandwell coming to Forsey's defence in the columns of *Saturday Night.* But Forsey needed no assistance. As Creighton wrote: "From the beginning, Dafoe was completely outclassed. In neither historical knowledge, legal erudition nor debating skills was he even remotely comparable to Eugene. He threshed about, like a huge, infuriated bull, tormented by the banderillas of Eugene's incisive style and pointed wit." According to a less partisan historian, Ramsay Cook: "No fair-minded reader of this exchange could fail to sympathize with Forsey's exasperation, nor doubt that Dafoe had met his master."

Forsey later wrote that Dafoe had "begun by accusing me of being part of a Tory conspiracy; he wound up by calling me a 'left-wing mudslinger and character assassin.'" Not for the last time, Forsey was baffling his adversaries by his apparent ideological inconsistencies, just as he would also perplex his allies. Later, after nearly three decades with the CCF, Forsey broke with its successor, the NDP, when the founding convention adopted a "two nations" policy for Quebec; like Creighton he regarded the policy as a travesty of history and constitutional tradition. In 1978, as a Liberal Senator, Forsey led the fight against the Liberal government's attempt to reform the constitution, calling the plan "revolutionary, subversive and an outrage against responsible government" and warning it would turn Canada into a republic. During the battle, he was accosted at lunch in the Chateau Laurier Grill by Trudeau's chief political aide, Jim Coutts. "Why are you doing this to us?" Coutts asked. Forsey looked at him scornfully: "Why are you doing this to the *country?*"

By now I was starting to sort out these apparent contradictions. For a start, Forsey always put his principles before any partisan allegiance. In turn, these principles grew out of what Creighton called "the two major intellectual enthusiasms of Eugene's career—his constitutional traditionalism and his social radicalism..." Since the former made him a conservative, while the latter clearly marked him as a socialist, it is understandable that Dafoe and others might be confused. Yet there is no philosophical inconsistency between the two enthusiasms. As Morton has shown, our British parliamentary traditions are a strong guarantee of social justice for all segments of society. In *Freedom and Order*, Forsey maintains time and time again that parliamentary government is the well-spring of our democracy, and perfectly amenable to the implementation of socialist policies.

But the confusion which Forsey has aroused goes deeper than any specious contradiction between his socialist and constitutional passions; it is based on the knee-jerk antipathy which the words 'conservative' and 'tory' arouse in so many liberals and leftists. For them the words conjure up a bloated, top-hatted capitalist intent on grinding down the poor and filling his pockets with the fruits of their toil. To the extent that he still exists, however, this caricature has nothing to do with our *indigenous* conservative tradition. Both the robber baron and his slicker successor, the contemporary "neo-conservative", are rightwing liberals: their natural habitat is the United States. As Morton has pointed out, the concept of free enterprise and rugged individualism was never the creation of conservatives: "As a doctrine it was a liberal invention and it bears the liberal trademark to this day." According to Grant, this American conservatism (or rightwing liberalism) has little connection to traditional conservatism, which grew out of British toryism of the pre-capitalist era, which was nurtured in Canada by the Loyalists, by French Canadian Catholics and by later generations of British immigrants, and which "asserts the right of the community to restrain freedom in the name of the common good." Unlike the caricatured capitalist, Canadian conservatives believe in an organic society and the mutual obligations among all classes. Which is why, like Morton, they embrace the principle of social justice and even the welfare state.

In *Arcadian Adventures of the Idle Rich,* one of his comic masterpieces. Leacock describes the tycoons of the imaginary City as they plot against each other with the sole object of increasing their fortunes. The slums in the suburbs are pointedly mentioned; just as pointedly, Leacock makes clear that the concerns of their inhabitants are far from the mind of the plutocrats of the Mausoleum Club (except when a strike of waiters sends them home without their dinners). *Arcadian Adventures* was published in 1914; in the immediate aftermath of World War One, Leacock's satiric vision seemed increasingly prophetic. Canadian business and industry were concentrated in the hands of a capitalist class many of whose members would have felt quite at home in the Mausoleum Club. Thousands of Canadians were leaving the countryside for the larger towns and cities, swelling the slums and increasing the social discontent brought on by the postwar recession, With the end of the earlier economic boom, business and labour became increasingly hostile. According to Alan Bowker: "Each class or group in society — women, returned soldiers, labourers, farmers, socialists, temperence men, religious revivalists, businessmen, scientists, intellectuals and politicians — came forward with a blueprint for Utopia which it pressed noisily, dogmatically, and sometimes violently." When the Winnipeg General Strike exploded into open conflict, many Canadians decided that the Bolshevik menace, already rampant in Europe, was now threatening their own security.

Amid the fear and confusion, Leacock proclaimed the need for "sane and serious thought". His own contribution was a series of articles which he wrote for the *New York Times* and published as a book in 1920. In *The Unsolved Riddle of Social Justice*, Leacock warned that it was time to re-examine the whole basis of Western political and economic organization: "If we do not mend the machine, there are forces moving in the world that will break it."

For a start Leacock recognized the appalling inequalities in Western society: "Riches and poverty jostle one another upon our streets. The tattered outcast dozes on his bench while the chariot of the wealthy is driven by." He noted that individualism—as proclaimed by classical economists and practised by venturesome businessmen—had provided the dynamic for modern industrialization; but individualism had failed to achieve the goal of social justice. At the same time he dismissed socialism as a practical alternative. Socialism was "a high and enobling idea truly fitted for a community of saints. And the one thing wrong with socialism is that it won't work."

Rejecting both utopian socialism and unchecked individualism, Leacock advocated a program of moderate reform. Society owed to every citizen the opportunity of a livelihood. Unemployment was a social crime; if necessary, work must be provided by the state. No nation could neglect its old and infirm; again the state must provide basic security. Above all, every child had a right to food, clothing, education and opportunity. To pay for these programs, Leacock would rely on "the terrific engine of taxation" already fashioned in the war: "Undoubtedly the progressive income tax and the tax on profits and taxation of inheritance must be maintained to an extent never dreamed of before." Social justice also depended on social legislation, such as laws fixing minimum wages and hours of work. But these reforms should take place within the private enterprise system: "The vast mass of human industrial effort must still lie outside of the immediate control of the government."

This is the program of a conservative with strong progressive tendencies: Leacock was ahead of his time in anticipating—and welcoming—the welfare state. In 1935 he wrote the introduction to Prime Minister Bennett's radio talk which advocated a Canadian New Deal to halt the Depression: again denouncing both socialism and *laissez-faire* liberalism, Leacock supported "the regulated state, preserving the stimulus of individual reward, but with a fairer set of rules to apply it." In one of his last books, *Our Heritage of Liberty* (1942), he rejected the liberal doctrine of essential freedom and its individualist ethic, while advocating the Burkean concept of an organic society based on order, discipline, hierarchy and mutual obligation. "True liberty ... liberty for all ... implies a sacrifice for each one of us of some of his rights in order that other people may have their rights too."

This theme of mutual obligation is central to the conservative tradition in Canada. As far back as 1872, Sir John A. Macdonald guided through Parliament his Trade Union Bills which established for the first time the rights and responsibilities of the burgeoning workers' movement. Significantly, the legislation was occasioned by a strike of Toronto printers whose most vociferous opponent was George Brown, publisher of the *Globe* and one of Macdonald's fiercest adversaries. Whereas Brown, a Grit, trumpeted the doctrine of free enterprise to justify his opposition to the strike, Macdonald had a broader vision and—according to Creighton—"a quick instinct for the kind of Tory democracy which Disraeli was to proclaim only a little later." If there was typical opportunism in Macdonald's move, there was also the tendency which Morton noted in Canadian conservatism: a willingness to move with the times when the need for change was proven.

Tory democracy—with its radical and populist strains—also appeared in that most aristocratic of Conservative leaders, Arthur Meighen. As Forsey wrote in 1960, on the occasion of his friend's death:

The missing note in the tributes has been that no one, as far as I have seen, has said anything about the radicalism with which he terrified the rank and fashion of the Conservative party in his early years, and which he never quite lost. To the present generation, Meighen was pre-eminently the defender of the status quo, the last hope of the stern and unbending Tories ... very few recall, or know, that he not only approved Bennett's New Deal of 1935, but piloted the bills through the Senate, and strengthened them in the process. He feared Socialism. He detested what he thought was the "Welfare State". But he was very far from being simply a doctrinaire "free enterpriser" or a "reactionary"; he nationalized three railways; and he was ready to support, and did support, any legislation which he was convinced would really promote welfare.

Now I could understand Morton's point that the true conservative is not restrained by ideology. He believes in tradition, authority and continuity (and his beliefs are often passionate), but he is also open to any change which promises to serve the general good. It was not only Meighen who nationalized three railways; Conservative governments also created the CPR, the Bank of Canada, the CBC and Ontario Hydro — in each case using public power to achieve national purposes. With this openness to public enterprise, the Canadian conservative bears little resemblance to that caricatured capitalist who trumpets the virtues of rugged individualism. Nor has he much to do with the neo-conservatism which became so fashionable in the Western world at the start of the nineteen-eighties. (Typically, Forsey dismissed the new doctrine as "just a fancy name for the biggest international romp ever mounted by the rich for skinning the poor.") But ... if the authentic Canadian conservative is neither a caricatured capitalist nor a neo-conservative ... then what *is* he? If he derives from an older and more socially responsible tradition, what form does that tradition take *today?* At this point, I was starting to reach some tentative conclusions. Specially, I was putting flesh on the bare bones of that strange creature, possibly endemic to Canada, the red tory.

Back in the nineteen-sixties, the political scientist Gad · Horowitz identified the native red tory in an essay which traced the historic affinities between Canadian conservatives and Canadian socialists, and stressed their common differences from North American liberals. Horowitz contended that it was wrong to dismiss Diefenbaker as an "aberration", as a prairie radical of the American type. Instead he found there had been an element of tory democracy or tory populism in the Conservative party since the time of Macdonald. Horowitz went on:

> Another "aberration" which is not really an aberration is the contemporary phenonemon of the red tory. At the simplest level, he is a Conservative who prefers the Co-operative Commonwealth Federation/New Democratic party to the Liberals, or a socialist who prefers the Conservatives to the Liberals, is a conscious ideological Conservative with some "odd" socialist notions (W. L. Morton) or a conscious ideological socialist with some "odd" tory notions (Eugene Forsey) . . . . . The tory and socialist minds have *some* crucial assumptions, orientations, and values in common, so that *from a certain angle* they may appear not as enemies but as two different expressions of the same basic ideological outlook. Thus, at the very highest level, the red tory is a philosopher who combines elements of toryism and socialism so thoroughly in a single integrated *Weltanschaung* that it is impossible to say that he is a proponent of either

one as *against* the other. Such a red tory is George Grant, who has associations with both the Conservative party and the NDP, defends Diefenbaker, laments the death of "true" British conservatism in Canada, attacks the Liberals as individualists and Americanizers, and defines socialism as a variant of conservatism (each "protects the public good against private freedom").

When I read Horowitz for the first time, some years ago, I found myself resisting the concept of red toryism. In those days I still considered myself a liberal, and my view of the political spectrum was conventional. Left was left, right was right, and the best path lay somewhere down the middle. Since I was also largely ignorant of Canadian history, I could only regard the red tory as an eccentric creature of no conceivable relevance, if not a logical impossibility.

By now, however, I knew differently. After meeting two of Horowitz's exemplars, I knew that red tories *do* exist, and that there is no necessary contradiction among the conservative, liberal and socialist components of their individual positions. Put simply, red tories are conservatives with a conscience. Respecting tradition and order they are also concerned with social justice and are willing to use public power to curtail private greed.

By now, too, I was feeling much less diffident about my own tendencies. Like Morton, Forsey was showing me that these were not necessarily a sign of incipient fascism, or senility, or both. Depending on the issue, a conservative could also be a liberal or even a radical: this meant that I could pursue my tendencies without having to regard *Globe and Mail* editorials as holy writ, or to accept William Davis as my mentor. Although the notion would seem heretical around Queen's Park and Bay Street, it also occurred to me that red tories might be the most authentic of Canadian conservatives, and that some form of red toryism might offer the best hope for our future.

I started thinking more about that future in the days that followed my first meeting with Forsey. I had staggered from his office—exhausted and exhilarated by the flood of anecdotes—with several questions still unasked. In particular, I had failed to get him talking about the United States. My own opinion was clear enough: there would be *no* hope for the future if Canada failed to assert its political, economic and cultural independence of the great republic. With one exception, the people I had seen, or intended to see, shared this concern: they were all nationalists who had spoken out strongly against the threat of American domination. The exception was Forsey. In searching the record, I found only a few occasions when he had appeared as a nationalist. In 1961, as an original member of the Board of Broadcast Governors, Forsey persuaded his fellow governors to reject an attempt by John Bassett to solve the financial problems of his new television station, CFTO, by bringing in ABC as a major shareholder. Later he wrote to *The Globe and Mail* in protest against the multitude of American text books in Ontario schools: "That children in any school in Ontario, of all places—a province founded by the United Empire Loyalists—and under a Conservative Government at that, should be stuffed with this all-American material, is scandalous and subversive." Despite such occasional outbursts, however, Forsey rarely considered the American threat in the nearly 200 articles and essays which he has published, and which deal mainly with economics and trade union matters, as well as the constitution. As Creighton wrote: "My Canadian nationalism was perhaps more prickly than Eugene's, his social awareness more sensitive than mine."

When I put this to him on our second meeting, Forsey agreed with Creighton's assessment. As partial explanation, he mentioned his trade union work: after leaving McGill in 1941, he became research director of the Canadian Congress of Labour and its successor, the Canadian Labour Congress, a post he held until 1966. In preparing a CLC brief for the Gordon Commission, he found no strong evidence that American ownership and control of our resources and our industries were a bad influence: "A lot of the talk was overdone." But Forsey also acknowledged that his trade union position had made it unlikely he would ever argue against any investment which provided jobs for workers. For once he sounded defensive, even apologetic. "It's a tricky subject," he said. "I've never gone into it thoroughly. I've had other preoccupations. I'm certainly a perfervid nationalist in constitutional and cultural matters. And I'm getting increasingly uneasy. I'm closer to Creighton and Grant than before."

It is true, of course, that Forsey's militant defence of our British traditions is an implicit nationalist stance, since these traditions embody many of our essential differences from the United States. Yet it seemed to me that Forsey's nationalism was compromised not only by his union allegiance, but also by his socialism. A socialist may have a strong sense of personal roots (this is certainly true of Forsey), but he also looks forward to a rosy future of international solidarity. This tends to make him less sensitive to incursions on national sovereignty. A conservative, on the other hand, is more concerned to protect his traditions against continental and international forces which threaten their particularity. As a leading exponent of left-wing nationalism, Abraham Rotstein, has written: "There is an important sense in which nationalism is inherently a conservative force; that is, it attempts to conserve and protect existing social institutions from outside penetration, in the name of the autonomy and self-determination of that society." In that context, I was closer to the conservative Creighton than the socialist Forsey, although I admired the latter's candid doubts about his stance.

In preparing for our second meeting, I had also come to

question Forsey's views on Quebec, and on the need for strong central government. This was tricky ground: over half a century, Forsey has established himself as *the* expert on Canadian constitutional matters. It is a fool-hardy politician, academic or journalist who gets his facts wrong, or evokes Forsey's militant concern for the perogatives of parliament: not only in his articles but also in scores of letters-to-the-editor, Forsey has rejoiced in demolishing the offenders with an angry wit. At times he has been guilty of rhetorical overkill. When the St. Laurent government began to replace the title "Dominion of Canada" with the simple "Canada", an exasperated Forsey charged: "The rot in our national life has gone so far that government thought it could safely unveil its treason." On other occasions he has indulged in heavy sarcasm. To proposals that the provinces receive sweeping powers at the expense of Ottawa, Forsey responded that the reconstituted nation would need "a distinctive flag, which would surely stir the blood of every citizen of the 10 mini-states: 10 jackasses eating leaves off a single maple tree." Like Creighton he has been accused of vilifying his adversaries, and Forsey himself concedes that he often gets carried away. "I'm endowed with a red hot English West Country temper," he told me. "I get so angry that my natural laziness is overcome." Somewhat to my surprise, I found him remorseful on the subject. "I've done more harm than good," he said with feeling. "I've hurt many people without a real excuse."

His anger peaked during the constitutional furor of the nineteen-seventies. In general, Forsey supported patriation of the constitution with an amending formula and a bill of rights, including minority language rights in all the provinces; he said he could also accept modest changes in the division of powers. But he rejected with contempt all proposals for sweeping decentralization. Ever since his boyhood trips to Parliament Hill, he had regarded the House of Commons as the great staging ground of Canadian democracy, and bitterly resented any attempts to limit its powers. When he supported Diefenbaker and the Conservatives, it was because they offered the only chance to end decades of Liberal arrogance and to repudiate the legacy of Mackenzie King, ("It is sometimes said that he put the people above Parliament," Forsey wrote of King. "That is not true. He put himself above both.") After Trudeau gained the Liberal leadership, Forsey backed him as the one leader who could hold the country together, and stave off demands from Quebec and other power-hungry provinces. Although Forsey never lost his admiration for Trudeau, he led the Senate fight against Trudeau's constitutional proposals of 1978, partly because he felt they would give the executive too much power at the direct expense of parliament. Yet Forsey was even more aghast when the Conservatives came to power, and Joe Clark proclaimed his vision of a "community of communities". Once again Forsey sounded the call for national unity. On the eve of the 1979 election, he made clear he would be supporting Trudeau. In a letter to *The Globe and Mail*, he warned:

> If the province-worshippers have their way, there will be no real Canada, just a boneless wonder. The province-worshippers would turn the clock back a hundred years or more. They would destroy the nation Cartier and Langevin, Brown and Macdonald, Tilley and Tupper, created. They would make us again a group of colonies, American colonies this time, with a life "poor, nasty, brutish and short."

In particular, Forsey fulminated against special status for Quebec. The loss of Quebec would be a tragic amputation, he maintained, but keeping Quebec within Canada by gutting the jurisdiction of parliament and by paralysing the central government would create a paraplegic. "If I have to choose, which God forbid, I should choose the amputee."

Like Creighton, Forsey has been accused of failing to understand the realities of French Canada. His support of the War Measures Act was seen by some critics as reactionary, especially on the part of a man who had been notably outspoken against Maurice Duplessis and his Padlock Law. Unlike Creighton, however, Forsey boasts of close ties with Quebec. For the last two decades, he has been an elder and a steward of a French Canadian United Church in Hull, and has often filled in for an absent minister, taking the service and even preaching the sermon. Forsey told me several anecdotes to show how he is often mistaken for a native French Canadian. "If I'm on my day I can get away with it, but I can just as easily make the most appalling boners. I'm more comfortable speaking French to less educated people. The higher educated French Canadian rather intimidates me." On one occasion, when complimented on his use of the subjunctive, Forsey replied: "You use the subjunctive a terrible lot in addressing the Deity."

Despite this background, Forsey's critics hold that he doesn't really understand French Canadians. According to a leading English Canadian academic, one of a group which has strongly supported greater concessions to Quebec, Forsey has become a destructive force, especially since he is a favourite of the media: "He hasn't moved with the times as Morton did. He presents an obdurate face to Quebec which only confirms them in their basic suspicion of us." Other critics contend that Forsey, like Creighton, has become much too rigid in his constitutional orthodoxy, and much too insensitive to the grievances and aspirations of all the regions. In his review of *Freedom and Order*, the historian Michael Cross charged that: "The essays stand as one of the best examples of the past generation of centralist interpretation, the Stonehenge of a vanishing view of Canada."

Already under the influence of Morton, I found myself ready to accept such criticisms. It still seemed crucial to maintain our British traditions, and especially to preserve the powers of the federal parliament. These are the essence of our democracy, and our surest protection against the arbitrary actions of cabinet ministers and civil servants. At the same time, I was starting to regard my centralist prejudices as selfish and short-sighted, a product of my Ontario background. I feared any further devolution for the obvious reason that it went too far, there might be nothing left to hold us all together, and to prevent our absorption by the United States. Like most Canadians, I was also thoroughly bemused by the intricacies of federal-provincial negotiations, and had little idea where the bargains should be struck. Much of the haggling seemed just that — it was so selfish and it showed so little vision that it made me wonder whether we had lost the will to reaffirm our sense of a Canadian community. Yet it seemed evident that Canada could survive only through completing a process of renewal that was already underway, and that would have to go further than an adamant centralist like Forsey could support. As Morton told me, when arguing for a reformed Senate with strong provincial representation: "I know this would send Eugene Forsey into a towering rage. I almost hope he's not around when it happens."

Near the end of our second interview, I broke into the flow of anecdotes long enough to ask Forsey to assess his achievements. For a moment, he was taken aback by the question — at once disturbed and thoughtful. "I don't think of myself as a very admirable character," he finally told me. "There have been too many failures of courage and judgment. I've done some awfully foolish things, and made too many sharp cracks." He thought some more. "I don't think I've accomplished very much. I've talked a certain amount of sense when a lot of nonsense was being talked by others. I wouldn't put it much higher than that." Finally, with a smile: "When people read my writings, they often say I'm brilliant. They think they've just seen the tip of the iceberg. They haven't. They've seen the whole thing!"

Those weren't, of course, his final words. Soon Forsey was wafting me out of his office and down the Senate corridors on a stream of further stories. His mandatory retirement was only weeks away, but it hardly fazed him: he had no intention of keeping silent while the "pygmies" tampered with his beloved constitution. Months later, as the patriation battle loomed large on Parliament Hill, Forsey was still in the midst of the fray. "The CBC wants me for the late-night wrap-up," he told a reporter cheerfully. "The old boy is still in demand."

It was another two years before I saw Forsey again. By then, the new constitution had been finally hammered out between Ottawa and nine of the ten provinces. On a cold winter evening in January, 1982, I went to hear Forsey give a public lecture on the subject at Toronto's Erindale College. There, inside an enormous concrete bunker, I found that Forsey was as perky and passionate as ever. I also found him damning the new constitution with the faintest of praise—and some typical barbs.

"Had I been in the Senate, I would have voted against it," Forsey declaimed. "I would have voted for the original version—before the provincial warlords got at it." In particular, he ridiculed "that ghastly 'notwithstanding' clause"—the clause that gives the provinces the power of opting out. "If you're going to have a charter of rights—on balance I'm for it, but not without reservations—it had better be entrenched." In fact, said Forsey, the new document offered the average citizen only a dubious protection for his rights. "The thing is badly drafted. Chances are it will take a very long time for the courts to determine what it means. The lawyers will have a field day. For them, it's a license to print money." Above all, putting the courts above parliament was creating

a very dangerous situation: "Judges should not mix themselves up in matters which are essentially political." At this
point, Forsey broke into a strained falsetto to sing a Gilbert
and Sullivan ditty mocking judges. Most of the audience—a
motley collection of academics and students— shuffled with
embarrassment. They seemed much too dutiful—failing to
catch, beneath the barbs and sallies, Forsey's deeper *gravitas*.

By now I was starting to suspect that Forsey really *hated*
the new constitution. But he did find one unexpected bonus
in the new document: "We now have the Monarchy, the
Governor-General, the Lieutenant-Governors remaining as
they are—*thoroughly entrenched* . . . . . Much of the dear old
Senate is also entrenched." Forsey paused for effect . . . now,
I knew, he was going to have some fun. "*And*—after all the
hullaballoo—the word 'Dominion' is still there!" Forsey was
waving his arms and spluttering with excitement. "*Dominion*!
It's meant to mean we're subservient—like monkeys on a
tree! *Well*—that never occurred to Sir John A., to Sir
George Etienne Cartier, to Sir Charles Tupper, to Sir
Wilfred Laurier, to Sir Robert Borden, to Arthur Meighen
or *even* to Mackenzie King!" (Here Forsey made a brief
digression to emphasize his deep abhorrence of King, but
also to establish that the assault on the term 'Dominion' came
during the era of St. Laurent.) Now he was positively
gloating: "This is one thing that the Grits overlooked—and
they'll have a horribly difficult time getting rid of it."

This was Forsey at his best . . . gleefully asperitous . . . a
termagant tory in hot-blooded defence of his cherished
traditions. Such, of course, has been his major contribution.
I could accept that Forsey was limited by a lack of vision:
like his conversation, his essays are precise and detailed and
studded with wicked barbs, but there is nothing there to
match the dramatic range of Creighton's histories or the bold
sweep of Morton's thought. ("Eugene's not a philosopher
at all," George Grant told me. "He's essentially a religious

man.") I could also agree that, as with Creighton, Forsey's thinking had remained too stubbornly centralist, and that he lacked sufficient sympathy for the aspirations of the different regions. But Forsey is important for his tough-minded defence of our monarchial and parliamentary traditions, and for his passionate insistence that these are the best guarantees of our democratic rights and any essential reforms. In all this, he has been a notable exemplar of the Canadian conservative tradition.

By now I was even more aware of the many strands to the tradition. At its best, it could encompass Morton's liberalism and Forsey's radicalism — as well as Purdy's folk-feelings — without compromising its basic tory slant. From the time of Macdonald, the conservative tradition was concerned with social justice, and so could easily embrace the phenomenon of the red tory. Rooted in the past, it was also open to the future — once again, I found that Burke had said it best:

> I cannot conceive how any man can have brought himself to that pitch of presumption, to consider his country as nothing but *carte blanche*, upon which he may scribble whatever he pleases. A man full of warm speculative benevolence may wish his society otherwise constituted than he finds it; but a good patriot, and a true politician, always considers how he shall make the most of the existing materials of his country. *A disposition to preserve, and an ability to improve, taken together, would be my standard of a statesman.* Everything else is vulgar in conception, perilous in the execution. [Emphasis added.]

Yet a deeper question remained. If Canadian tories came in many authentic guises ... if their different passions comprised a conservative tradition that was rich and vital ... was that tradition still relevant, or was it doomed to demise? At this point, I still didn't know. But I *did* know it was time to confront the brooding philosopher who had proclaimed that conservatism was no longer a possibility in our era.

VI
Threnody:
George Grant

Before they moved back to Halifax, George and Sheila Grant lived for many years in Dundas, a suburb of Hamilton. To get there from Toronto, you drive along the Queen Elizabeth Way through the heartland of industrial Ontario: mile after mile of clean, well-groomed factories, spaciously set and neatly landscaped. Eventually you pass McMaster, where Grant taught for two decades, but if it wasn't for the sign, you'd hardly know it as a university: mammoth and functional, it looks more like a sibling to the Ford complex in Oakville, or some ultra-efficient power plant. Finally you drive through a glut of shopping plazas—acres of asphalt and the garish neon lights of fast-food emporiums. Each time I took this route, I felt I was being engulfed by both the crass modernity and the dehumanizing technology which Grant has described as compromising our particular fate. It was always a relief to leave the main road—turning off beside a cluster of ranchstyle and mock-Tudor bungalows— and to enter the Grants' small rural enclave.

My first visit took place during a federal election campaign: both of the limestone gate-pillars were adorned with blue Conservative posters. At the end of the curving dirt drive, the house loomed up with stolid dignity amid a chaos of tangled trees, plump bushes, wild flowers and unkempt lawns. Much like the Creighton home in Brooklin, it was another century-old Ontario farm house of mellowed red-and-white brick, rising to a strong central dormer. Somewhat askew, with fading paint and cracking plaster, it looked like a dowager down on her luck, but still redoubtable. The house seemed to grow there, rooted in the land, with the surrounding foliage as a bulwark against the encroachment of the clamorous highway and all those flashy bungalows.

Clearly the enclave was besieged. And, on my last visit, I found the Grants in the midst of a strategic retreat. Grant had accepted a teaching post at Dalhousie and had prefaced the move with an article in *The Globe and Mail*, assailing the way in which universities such as McMaster had become gigantic knowledge factories emphasizing research over teaching, technical excellence over the dialectical pursuit of truth. Now there were large wooden packing cases in the corridors, and the house was beginning to be bare. But enough furniture remained in the living room to recall the home as it had been. It was a low-keyed but eloquent assortment: a bulbous, baroquish secretary-chest-of-drawers, a plump *chaise-longue*, a puritanesque New England-style armchair, a low-slung Nova Scotian rocker, a rococco gilt screen, an Oriental rug, a medley of florid cups and saucers on the mantlepiece, and—on the walls—prints and pictures which convoked the larger world of Athens, Rome and China. In actual style, nothing was the same, but everything seemed bourgeois Victorian in feeling, as well as date. Nothing was terribly fine, yet nothing was merely cheap. And all was agreeably, comfortably lived with, and dilapidated. As the novelist Scott Symons described the scene: "IT WAS

ALL THERE... the entire reality of my culture... with roots back to Britain, to Europe, to the East. It was all there, intact, restored to me, rumpling and rampaging all around us... my own culture and heritage as an Ontarian (in sharp contrast to the kempt, mod-con world outside)... not just bits and pieces of it, not just some academic recollection of it... but the whole damned bloody wondrous thing, rich and snorting and gentle and tough and stern and affection-ate and intimate and august... ALL THERE!"

I had brought Symons with me, as well as Dennis Lee, the poet and editor. Each of us had been touched by Grant; each of us had become involved in his concerns. (Grant had spoken out in support of my books and he wrote the preface to Symons' furniture book, *Heritage*. Lee had edited Grant's *Technology and Empire*.) The bonds were strong, and Grant had asked us down for a farewell visit which was almost a ceremonial leave-taking to mark a crucial stage in his own work. (As he had told me in a letter: "I am hoping in Nova Scotia to get away from the silly involvement in McMaster which has stood in the way of thinking.") In honour of the occasion, we had armed ourselves with gifts from the Rare Wine Store: a couple of fine German Ausleses and a majestic Marc de Bourgogne de Corton Grancy.

We talked for five tumultuous hours. Sheila Grant—a statuesque, white-haired woman with a regal bearing and a ready wit—sat in one of the arm chairs. There was nothing regal about George as he presided from the *chaise-longue*, although he was even more monumental. Grant is a burly man with an impressive corporation, but what you really notice is the massive head and shaggy beard. (He'd be splendid in a toga.) For a man in his sixties, his face is youthful—lined but not wrinkled. His full head of brown hair is brushed and parted, although not quite tidy. Even in a suit, Grant appears rumpled and dishevelled. All in all, he often suggests an overgrown schoolboy trying to be proper, but not fully succeeding. His voice has traces of an English accent: neither very loud nor very deep, it *feels* both loud and deep, something like an organ. When Grant talks, he clenches himself up, drawing all his strength together, takes a deep breath and then the words bellow out. He leans into his sentences: the key phrases explode amid a flurry of arms and hands.

That afternoon our conversation ranged from bird watching to the split between the Roman and Orthodox Churches, from Saint Augustine to Vincent Massey. Grant had recently discovered the French novelist Céline, and was full of praise for his books — especially the later war novels — if not for his fascist philosophy. "He's colossal... a colossal genius! He makes Joyce look like two cents. And Sartre... that third-rate thinker, third-rate writer... Céline is so much greater. I just don't see how such a great artist could have such evil ideas." He pauses, then adds more quietly: "I started to read Céline when I was feeling down. I felt I was on the edge of a nervous breakdown..." Sheila breaks in affectionately: "Oh, George is always on the brink of one nervous breakdown or another. Usually he goes and reads the biography of some Anglican Bishop."

By now Sheila is presiding over tea and sandwiches, while Grant is deep in recollection. "Pouring tea was terribly important, you know. I remember one of those family occasions. The tea-pourer had to leave the room for just a minute. One of the other guests filled in. She was triumphant about it afterwards. 'I just couldn't *resist* pouring,' she apologized. That's what it was like in Toronto in the nineteen-forties. Whoever poured the tea was *very* important." Grant quakes with delight, and looks to see whether we've grasped the point. "I mean it's changed *that much* since then." He lurches to his feet and lumbers to the table for a second cup, refusing to let his wife bring it to him, a courtly gesture to the pourer-of-the-tea.

Before long we have finished the tea and are into the Ausleses. At first, Grant makes a mock protest. "I can't drink wine in the afternoon. There's too much of the English shopkeeper in me for that." But he finally consents to a glass, and another, and then we venture on to the Marc, that most robust of the brandies. Grant peers at his glass warily, then takes a gingerly sip. "You're trying to *debauch* me!" he shouts, clutches his arms about him, and detonates with laughter.

Eventually we are back on weightier topics. A discussion of the Christian Eucharist leads to a statement that the Canadian identity is predicated on a denial of all such passions. Grant agrees, with reservations. "But it's the whole Western world, not just Canada. The story of the West is the story of *will*. Will governing the passions, and often ruling against life." He ponders some more. "Yet you'd be wrong to think that Canadians have no passion. They have a *huge* passion . . ." he raises his arms, opening them wide, " . . . to make money. MONEY!" he roars. "They stop at nothing. Families break up. Children are neglected. For the sake of more money. I find it . . . *awesome*. But it's there . . . a huge, cold, intense passion . . ."

Time and time again, we return to Apollo and Dionysius, the presiding gods of our encounter. "I *like* this," Grant says, sipping at the Marc, his eyes glinting with pleasure. (At that moment there is nothing of the school boy about him, and little of the monumental magus. For a few seconds the face and body are something off a Greek vase . . . a veritable Silenus.) "Yes," he continues, "I'm a natural Dionysian. I can't finish my sentences, sometimes can't even start them . . . . . I could have given way so easily, to minor forms of Dionysianism. But I'm a very basic Protestant. For me, thought is redemptive. You see, I've fought all my life to be Apollonian . . . *all my life!*" He pauses, starts to laugh, wheezing through his cigarette, ashes spewing down his ample front. "But I'm enormously Dionysian, ENORMOUSLY!" His whole body quakes with laughter, a laughter that is some sort of raging giggle. "And yet," he adds, checking himself and speaking with great firmness, "Apollo is primary!"

Soon we are on to saints, especially the French Christian philosopher Simone Weil. Grant has called her the greatest influence on his thought. ("She has shown me how sanctity and philosophy can be at one.") He has also insisted on his limitations—as a thinker and as a moral being—which restrict his ability, and his right, to speak of ultimate matters. Now he is pondering a question about the nature of modern sainthood. "Well... Simone Weil... *her* life... I mean, when she says Christ visited her, came down to her, I have to believe her. I have to know that did happen..." Grant pauses, muses, his lower lip thrust forward. He has reached some line, some point beyond which he cannot move. Finally he sighs: "It has taken all my energy just to understand what virtue might be, the nature of a virtuous life..."

Near the end of our five hours, Grant says suddenly: "Do you know, the whole Occidental experience may be a failure? Has it never struck you? I mean, I got up one morning recently, and was having my coffee. And it occurred to me that the whole Western experiment may now be a mistake. I asked Sheila what she thought..." Grant just tosses out the comment. Lee chortles: "Imagine having *that* thrown to you over breakfast!" Grant nods and rocks with laughter. "Oh, Sheila was very good. She thought about it carefully..." Now we are all laughing. It's so bizarre, this momentous statement just dropping on us, almost as an afterthought, yet carrying the entire weight of our afternoon. Implicit in everything we have been discussing, yet none of us explicitly aware of it. As we get to our feet, and prepare to depart, Grant is still wrestling with the idea. "Don't you see, the Western world might *well* be a failure now..."

Philosophy must arise from the most immediate and concrete experience of our lives, both public and private. I never forget returning home to

Toronto after many years in Halifax. Driving in from the airport, I remember being gripped in the sheer presence of the booming, pulsating place which had arisen since 1945. What did it mean? Where was it going? What had made it? How could there be any stop to its dynamism without disaster, and yet, without a stop, how could there not be disaster? And part of that experience was the knowledge that I had come home to something that could never be my home. Philosophy arises in the wonder of such lived experiences.

[From *George Grant in Process.*]

George Grant has always been the most public of philosophers. If his thinking leads him to speculate on the ultimate meaning of the whole Western experience, it is also rooted in his particular situation as a Canadian living in the second half of the twentieth century, and his need to communicate his perceptions and his fears. Some of his earliest essays dealt with Canada's position at the end of World War Two. His most famous book, *Lament for a Nation*, was written in the midst of a federal election campaign and was abruptly dismissed by several critics as an improbable defence of the impossible Diefenbaker. The essays in *Technology and Empire* were suffused with Grant's despair over the American intervention in Vietnam; as he said in the preface, it was a time when the English-speaking world had reached its basest point. More recently, his musings on the nature of justice return, again and again, to his horror at the growing tolerance of abortion.

"You have to live *in* the world," Grant told me. "I can't imagine *not* living in the world. Sheila and I have raised six children. I can't imagine not having a family. You learn so much."

Instead of confining himself to writing for fellow academics in scholarly journals, Grant has more often addressed a wider public over the CBC, or in popular magazines and newspapers. Unlike many of his colleagues, he is concerned to be understood. "I'm contemptuous of modern academia," he told me. "All those pompous charlatans ... most write very poorly." Like his conversation, Grant's prose is pungent, if sometimes ponderous, and his essays abound in references to such public figures as Bing Crosby, J. D. Salinger, Billy Graham and E. P. Taylor. He is a master of the vivid aphorism. ("One is tempted to state that the North American motto is: 'the orgasm at home and napalm abroad.' ") If he sometimes uses difficult words like 'autochthonous', his favourite epithet is 'slick' (as in "Trudeau is a slicky").

Above all, Grant has spoken out clearly and directly on the future which confronts Canadians. In *Lament for a Nation* and his later essays, he has developed a devastating account of how the forces of liberal technology are absorbing Canada and other countries in a universal and homogeneous state which threatens mankind with an overwhelming tyranny. As Grant sees it, only an enlightened conservatism might preserve traditional values of justice and freedom, but conservatism is impotent in the face of such an all-pervasive liberalism. Hence Canada — or any such "local culture" — is doomed to disappear. "The impossibility of conservatism in our era is the impossibility of Canada," Grant wrote near the end of *Lament*.

This, of course, is why I had to tackle Grant. For if he is accurate in his analysis, it means that the conservative tradition, despite its vitality and diversity, is doomed to extinction. If Grant is right, moreover, it means that none of us — conservatives, socialists or liberals — has any real choice but to acquiesce in the gradual demise of our nation. In that case, this book would be an exercise in futility, and little more than a personal footnote to Grant's much greater threnody.

It may seem ironic (or simply appropriate), but the man who proclaimed the death of an independent Canada is the direct descendent of two prominent Victorians who predicted a triumphant destiny for their young nation. George Parkin Grant is the grandson of George Munro Grant and Sir George Parkin. Both were leaders among the Canadian Imperialists. We have already encountered Parkin as the mentor of Leacock and the "wandering evangelist of Empire". Of Scottish descent, George Munro Grant—who was widely known as Principal Grant for his long tenure as head of Queen's University—was no less influential as a fellow nationalist, and no less ready to identify the progress of mankind with the spread of Anglo-Saxon civilization. A vigorous Presbyterian preacher, Principal Grant declared in 1890 that Canada's destiny was to be "a link that shall bind into a world-wide brotherhood, into a moral—it may be a political—unity the mother of all nations, and all her children, the greater daughter to the south of us as well as the youngest born of the family." On other occasions, Grant was less friendly to the United States, warning of its political and territorial aspirations, and contrasting American and British values to the advantage of the latter. For all his nationalist fervor, however, Principal Grant embodied a Protestant activism which helped to prepare Canadians for their eventual adherence to the empire of liberal technology. "Work! Honest work for and with God in Christ!" Grant trumpeted to a Presbyterian Synod in 1866. "This is the Gospel that is preached on to us. No form, new or old, no pet doctrine or panacea, nor institution or catechism can take the place of that." As his grandson was to note, this identification of Christianity with practicality led to the glorification of personal power and social engineering. In the twentieth century, these became ends in themselves: "But always the control of the world is seen as essentially moral."

Grant never knew his grandfathers. Born in 1918, the youngest of four children, he was raised in Toronto where his father was headmaster of Upper Canada College. William Grant died when his son was entering his teens, and the dominant influence on the young man was his mother. One of the first women to graduate from McGill, and later head of its Royal Victoria College, she was formidable. According to Eugene Forsey: "Maude Parkin could have run the British Empire with one hand tied behind her back—and run it well!" Grant describes his mother as a secularized Protestant who didn't believe a word of Christianity. Instead she believed in progress. "She was an improver. Perhaps that's why I've never found improvers easy. Mr. Leacock would come to our house and father would get him to swear—just to annoy mother. Once we were walking past an imposing building in Montreal and my mother said with great disapproval: 'You know, Mr. Leacock spends his *life* in that club.'" Grant sighed. "It was hard to be her son."

Growing up in Toronto also presented difficulties. Grant says he hated UCC, partly because his father was headmaster, and partly because he was bad at sports. (Perhaps in retaliation, he joined a small cell of fledgling socialists.) Gradually he became aware of deeper problems, in particular the spiritual and sensual deprivations which Toronto society imposed upon its members. Much later, he would write that "for myself it has taken the battering of a lifetime of madness to begin to grasp even dimly that which has been inevitably lost in being North American." He was brought up in an atmosphere of secular liberalism; his elders could no longer believe in the Christianity of their parents, so they adopted goals and standards which were resolutely pragmatic. What he missed was any concern for deeper values, for the contemplation and creativity which he began to sense were part of his broader European heritage. Sexuality was also denied, or at least suppressed. "I grew up hating my body," he told me. "For a long time that produced chaos and disorder in my life. In that atmosphere of secularized Calvinism, the ecstatic was excluded. There was no place for sexual, religious or aesthetic ecstasy. Ecstasy! I just want to lick my lips when I say that word!" Grant recalls attending performances of Mozart at Hart House, under the auspices of his uncle, Vincent Massey. "Everyone just sat there—very dutifully. There was Uncle Vincent putting on the Hart House Quartet, and no one was enjoying it!" (Later, Mozart would become one of Grant's greatest passions.) It was made clear that the young Grant was to emulate his distinguished ancestors by finding a useful place in public life. "My mother had totally programmed me for ambition." After the war, when Grant told his mother he was going to study philosophy, she replied: "George—you have always been the *poseur* of the family, but this is the worst pose of all!"

By then, however, Grant had already broken free. War provided the crucial experiences. At its outbreak he was at Oxford studying history, politics and law on a Rhodes Scholarship. Because he was a pacifist, he joined the Air Raid Precaution service, and was posted to the Bermondsey dockyard area in London's east end. At the height of the Blitz, he was working day and night, going long periods without sleep. Often hundreds of people were killed in a single raid. Grant soon discovered that the secular liberalism of his youth could not come to terms with all that horror. "Violence was happening all the time," he told me. "It liberated me. It totally broke the pattern my mother had imposed. I really began to live poetically. The ecstatic side of my nature came out." (Here he gave a shout of affirmation.) Later Grant joined the Merchant Marine, but after contracting tuberculosis he went to the English countryside to work on a farm. Then he had another breakthrough."I went to work at five o'clock in the morning on a bicycle. I got off the bicycle to open a gate and when I got back on I accepted God." Grant had a sudden conviction that—beyond space and time—there was order. Later he would say: " . . . it was the recognition that I was not my own.

In more academic terms, if modern liberalism is the affirmation that our essence is our freedom, then this experience
was the denial of that definition, before the fact that we are
not our own." Grant never came to doubt the truth of that
epiphany: it would always sustain him. As he told me:
"Christianity was now part of the ecstasy."

I listened to all this in some confusion: Grant's saga
sounded so particular, yet also very familiar. Although I was
younger than Grant, his boyhood Toronto was not all that
different from mine: I, too, had felt baffled and dispirited
amid similar constraints. It did not surprise me that Grant
had broken free only when he went abroad: this had been
my experience and it has been common, during much of this
century, to a large number of Canadian artists and writers.
In our different ways, we were all fleeing a narrow, secular
society which was devoted to the liberal ideals of progress
and improvement, and which was frightened by both sensual-
ity and spirituality. With most of us, it was not a matter of
merely going native in some distant land, or losing ourselves in some foreign creed. Rather, it was a matter of
exploring those life-enhancing insights which are natural to
older civilizations and which are part of our human heritage. In seeking to reclaim that heritage, we were enacting an
impulse which I now recognize as fundamentally conservative.

In my case it was not only Europe, but also Asia and
Africa which had helped me to comprehend the limitations
of my secular Canadian society. Unlike Grant, however, I
had not discovered God in the course of my travels. As a
closet conservative, I had been stirred by some of the great
spiritual statements of those older civilizations. It was always
exhilarating, for instance, to stand before the blue-domed
splendour of the Temple of Heaven in Peking, and to absorb
its proud assertion of man's place within a universal order.
By the time I came to tackle Grant, I knew that a conservative *must* finally acknowledge the existence of some such
order — the belief is as implicit in Purdy as it was explicit in

Morton. In my case, however, this belief was the product of mere mind: I had never had a mystical experience of the Diety, or whatever term might best define that higher intelligence. I knew it was there, but I hadn't felt it. Clearly this would limit my ability to fathom Grant, although it did not inhibit me from plunging into the more political aspects of his thought.

Apart from the release of his late-blooming ecstasy, the war left Grant with an overwhelming sense of horror at the ruin it had wrought. In essays which he published in 1945, he tried to find some basis on which the peace might be preserved. Grant foresaw that the United States and the Soviet Union were developing great regional empires which would hinder the United Nations from establishing a new order. Only the Commonwealth, with its world-wide interests and membership, could prevent regional isolation and future strife; although decentralized, it still had "enough unity within itself to stand as a power between these two colossi." As a leading member of the Commonwealth, Canada was especially well placed to exert a continuous pressure on the United States to avoid isolationism and take its proper place in the new order: "Here the choice is ours and it will be a choice that will effect the whole world."

His grandfathers would have approved such a robust assertion of a special Canadian role. And, as we have seen, Leacock and Creighton had been writing in a similar vein. Like them, Grant failed to foresee the rapid decline of Britain as a world power, and the centrifugal forces which would eventually paralyse the Commonwealth. Like them, too, he overestimated Canada's ability to influence the United States. Much more than Leacock and even Creighton, however, Grant already had a strong apprehension of American threats to Canadian independence. It was these threats—not any attachment to the past—which made it imperative for Canada to preserve its Commonwealth links: "The basic reason why we are not part of the U.S.A. is because we have remained in the British orbit." But a close alliance with Britain and the Commonwealth would not in itself guarantee our continued independence: "It must be categorically stated that Canada will only continue to exist as long as we represent something individual and special in ourselves." Again there was an echo of his grandfathers when Grant described these special features as being based on the historic maintenance of Canada's ties with Britain: "This meant first of all that we were a conservative nation . . . . . Second, this origin of our country has meant that we are a society where social order is of prime importance." Here Grant was starting to sound that concern for conservative traditions which made Canada both socially and morally distinct from the great republic:

> Unless we have our own national way, we will have the American way. If we bow prostrate before the culture of Hollywood; if in education we accept from the south the phoney precepts of so-called 'progressive education'; if socially we welcome in our Granite Clubs the Babbitry of the middle west and the intolerance of the deep south; if economically we accept the uncontrolled individualism of American business and call it British freedom; if our entertainment criterion is Frank Sinatra and philosophically and religiously we accept the materialist claptrap from the USA— then we will in effect have given up those values that are essentially Canadian and we might as well become part of Leviathan. Morally and intellectually we will have become a colony of the republic and should therefore ask for admission to the union.

It is clear enough what Grant disliked about the liberal American way of life; it is less evident what he thought should be the conservative Canadian alternative. Obviously he was not recommending the repressive regimen which he had known as a youth, nor was he suggesting that Canadians should merely ape British ways. With the benefit of hindsight, Grant's disgust at the grosser elements in American life foreshadows not only his continuing preoccupation with the threats to Canadian independence, but also his subsequent concern with deeper philosophical questions. There are glimmerings—in his attacks on the "uncontrolled individualism" and the "materialistic claptrap"—of that yearning for the good which would come to dominate his later writings. At this point, however, Grant could hardly be more specific since he had only begun to explore the basic differences between the Canadian conservative and the North American liberal traditions. Moreover, he still retained some liberal tendencies of his own, including a modified belief in historical progress, which complicated his perception of those differences. Above all, Grant in 1945 had still to develop his theory of modern technology—that inexorable force which, he would later say, had made inevitable Canada's absorption in the American empire.

Grant's fears of American domination were heightened during the remarkable period of postwar business expansion: here again, his philosophy grew in part out of "lived experiences". After postgraduate studies at Oxford, he joined the philosophy department at Dalhousie in 1947. In his book, *Philosophy in the Mass Age*, published in 1959, he remarked on how the chain stores, the automobile companies and other great business enterprises had established a continental domain. "I, for instance, live in a little peninsula on the fringes of Canada which two generations ago had a rather simple but intelligible agricultural, commercial, and military culture of its own. Even in the ten short years I have lived in Halifax, I have watched with amazement the speed with which the corporation empires have taken over this old culture and made it their own. This culture of monolithic capitalism creates the very fabric of all our lives."

Grant saw this new North American society as the incarnation of the liberal idea that man was the maker of all progress, and the master of his total environment. In turn, this led him to elaborate his own conservative stance. As he went on to maintain, ancient philosophers had viewed man as part of a natural order, and as subject to divine law, whereas the modern philosophy of liberalism placed him in full control of his destiny. For Grant, this posed a dilemma: "The question thoughtful people must ask themselves is whether the progressive spirit is going to hold within itself any conception of spiritual law and freedom; or whether our history-making spirit will degenerate into a rudderless desire for domination on the part of our elites, and aimless pleasure among the masses." In later years, Grant would ask this question with increasing urgency and a sense of impending doom; at this point, he was still capable of restrained optimism. On balance he felt that the benefits of technology outweighed the defects, since modern man had been liberated from the practical demands of sheer survival. But Grant was divided in his mind about the relations between the moral traditions of the West and the new religion of progress. As he stated in an introduction to a later edition of the book:

> Some glimmering of what it was to believe in an eternal order had been vouchsafed to me so that I was no longer totally held by the liberal faith. I believed in a moral order which men did not measure and define but by which we were measured and defined. At the practical level, I had seen many of the limitations of the technological society. Nevertheless, I was still held by the progressive dogma. It is hard indeed to overrate the importance of faith in progress through technology to those brought up in the main stream of North American life.

Here Grant was grappling with a dilemma which confronts all conservatives. Whether or not they have glimpsed an eternal order, conservatives believe in tradition and continuity; the mad rush of technological advance leaves them bemused and apprehensive; they simply cannot accept the liberal notion that progress is automatically good, and that the new is inherently superior to the old. Yet conservatives also have to recognize that science and technology have brought many benefits to mankind: there is no point in lapsing into wistful reaction, harking back to some mythical golden age and blaming modernity for all the current social ills. "Only a false mediaevalism can paint the past in colours superior to the present," Leacock wrote in *Social Justice* and then went on to advocate a reform program which was well ahead of its time. As we have also seen with Morton, the true conservative is open to any change which seems to serve the general welfare. What he hates is progress for the sake of progress, progress as religion.

Similarly Grant. In *Philosophy in the Mass Age*, he was not asserting that ancient cultures were better than our own: "It is only necessary to think what modern men have done to make life pleasant, to cut down the curses of pain and work (and they are curses) to see how great the achievements of the modern world have been." What bothered Grant was the total freedom which liberalism gives to modern man. "Surely the twentieth century has presented us with one question above all: are there any limits to history making? The question must be in any intelligent mind whether man's domination of nature can lead to the end of human life on the planet, if not in a cataclysm of bombs, perhaps by the slow perversion of the processes of life." Grant's answer—in part—was to assert the existence of a moral law which limits man's freedom: "The idea of God, having been discarded as impossible and immoral, comes back in the twentieth century as men recognize that if there is no theoretical limit there is no practical limit, and any action is permissible."

Here I was plunged into a dilemma of my own. I could accept Grant's account of the dangers of unlimited liberalism, but I could not envisage how — in such a secular era — the ideas of God and a moral law could ever regain their former importance. I was not impressed by such contemporary phenomena as the Moral Majority and the surge of television evangelism, since these had less to do with genuine faith than with social repression and sheer hucksterism. Nor did I find much evidence of a deep-rooted spiritual revival in the antics of the saffron-robed Hare Krishnas, chanting through the streets, or among the multitudes who follow such flamboyant gurus as Maharaji Ji and the Rev. Moon. Grant, of course, was far from advocating such singular and superficial paths, nor was he propagating any specific Christian doctrine. But if the idea of God *was* coming back to us, I could not see it taking hold in any lasting manner.

On a practical level, however, I could follow Grant more readily when he argued that conservatism was the best antidote to the liberal doctrine of unlimited progress: "The truth of conservatism is the truth of order and limit, both in social and personal life . . . . . there can be no doubt that we all have need of a proper conservatism, an order which gives form to persons, to families, to education, to worship, to politics, and to the economic system." This had echoes of Leacock and Morton, and it was close to my own inclinations. But it also landed Grant in a further dilemma, as he quickly conceded: "Yet to express conservatism in Canada means *de facto* to justify the continuing rule of the business man and the right of the greedy to turn all activities into sources of personal gain. The conservative idea of law has often been in the mouths of capitalists, but seldom in their actions."

At this stage — shortly before Horowitz described him as the highest sort of red tory — Grant's thinking is suffused with elements of conservatism, liberalism and socialism. All three are present in "An Ethic of Community", a major essay

which was published in 1961, although socialism predomin-
ates. Grant acknowledges the conservative principle of
hierarchy—which arises from a diversity of talents—but says
this must be balanced against the principle of equality—
which arises from the absolute worth of all men. Asserting
that Canadian governments, both Liberal and Conservative,
have always identified their interests and the interests of
Canada with those of the business elite, Grant goes on to
state that there can be no major attack on social injustice
within the framework of a capitalist system. At the same
time, he admonishes socialists not to indulge in the same
immoral politics as Liberals and Conservatives, and not to
adopt a vague and innocent ethic which deals in material
rewards and is based on a simple belief in progress.

Yet Grant himself still had some faith in progress. His
essay concludes with the optimistic assertion that "North
America is the first continent called upon to bring human
excellence to birth throughout the whole range of the
technological society." That was in 1961. Five years later—
when he wrote the introduction to a new edition of *Philosophy in the Mass Age*—Grant's views had undergone a
dramatic change: "I no longer believe that technology is
simply a matter of means which men can use well or badly.
As an end in itself, it inhibits the pursuit of other ends in the
society it controls. Thus, its effect is debasing our conceptions of human excellence."

It is this new perception—rather than Grant's anguish over
the defeat of Diefenbaker—which provides the deeper basis
of *Lament for a Nation* (1965). Grant had been studying the
American political scientist Leo Strauss and the French
social critic Jacques Ellul and had come to agree with them
that liberal technology was leading Western man not to
greater freedom and excellence, but to eventual enslavement within a universal and homogeneous state. For Grant,

this state is the pinnacle of all political striving in the modern era: "Where modern science has achieved its mastery, there is no place for local cultures." With relentless logic, he argues why Canada, one of those local cultures, has to disappear. "First, men everywhere move ineluctably toward membership in the universal and homogeneous state. Second, Canadians live next to a society that is the heart of modernity. Third, nearly all Canadians think that modernity is good, so nothing essential distinguishes Canadians from Americans."

On this basis, Grant builds his angry account of the more particular reasons for Canada's collapse. ("This lament mourns the end of Canada as a sovereign state.") Although he is scathing about Diefenbaker's failings, he sees the prairie populist as the last champion of Canadian nationalism — a flawed, quixotic figure who was brought down by the combined forces of the political, business and civil service elites, all firmly committed to continentalism. These were the forces of liberalism, and Grant now sees liberalism as an inexorable force. It was always futile to argue (as he once did) that other traditions and doctrines might have deflected its dynamism and preserved an independent Canadian nation. As far back as the carnage of World War One, Britain had lost the power to remain an alternative pull in Canadian life. Although Britain provided Canada with distinctive legal and political traditions, there is no deep division of principle between these and American institutions, and no radically different approach to the questions of industrial civilization. "Certainly none of the differences between the two sets of institutions are sufficiently important to provide the basis for an alternative culture on the northern half of this continent." Grant finds the French tradition in Canada to be more formidable, and he is sympathetic to French Canadian aspirations. But the reality of their culture, and their desire not to be swamped, cannot save French Canadians from the relentless pull of continentalism. While they want to preserve their culture, they also want the benefits of progress. These are contradictory goals: "Nationalism can only be asserted successfully by an identifiction with technological advance; but technological advance entails the disappearance of those indigenous differences that give substance to nationalism."

Turning to political traditions, Grant argues that the drift to economic integration with the United States could have been restrained after 1940 only through strong government planning and controls: a combination of nationalism and socialism. But this, too, was an impossible dream. For a start, socialism, — like conservatism — involves restraints on individual freedom for the sake of the general good. But most Canadians are committed to the religion of progress and emancipated passions; to them, corporation capitalism is a much more suitable regime. Grant also blames the "good-natured utopians" who have led our socialist parties: "They had no understanding of the dependence of socialism and nationalism in the Canadian setting. Their confused optimism is seen in the fact that they have generally acted as if they were 'left-wing' allies of the Liberal party . . . . . Such a doctrine was too flaccid to provide any basis for independence."

Likewise conservatism: another "impossible" ideology in our era. Because technology and science produce such a dynamic society, nothing can be conserved for long: all institutions and standards are constantly changing. "Conservatives who attempt to be practical face a dilemma. If they are not committed to a dynamic technology, they cannot hope to make any popular appeal. If they are so committed, they cannot hope to be conservatives." In this situation, conservatives can only advocate a sufficient amount of order so that the demands of technology will not carry the society into chaos. Which is not, Grant indicates, the most stirring or popular of roles. It is a role that is also doomed to futility:

> The impossibility of conservatism in our era is the impossibility of Canada. As Canadians we

attempted a ridiculous task in trying to build a
conservative nation in the age of progress, on a
continent we share with the most dynamic nation
on earth. The current of modern history is against
us.

When *Lament for a Nation* was published, I was still living
abroad: I read it for the first time only on my return to
Canada in the early nineteen-seventies. I was puzzled by my
initial reaction. I found it impossible to resist the force of
Grant's argument and the sweep of his prose. Logically, I
should have been plunged into despair: if my country was
being inexorably drawn into the American empire, then
what was the point in my return? Yet *Lament* did not make
me despondent: just the opposite, since I found it exhilarating. This paradox was difficult to explain, but it seemed that
others had a similar reaction. According to the socialist Jim
Laxer: "It's the most important book I ever read in my life.
Here was a crazy old philosopher of religion at McMaster
and he woke up half our generation. He was saying Canada
is dead, and by saying it he was creating the country."
    Grant had indeed woken us up. Soon I became aware
that his book had become a Bible for younger nationalists,
whether we called ourselves conservatives, socialists or even
liberals. Somehow he had shaken us out of our lethargy and
made us determined to prove him wrong. His jeremiad was
compelling, but we stubbornly refused to concede that all
was inevitably lost. In the introduction to a new edition of
Lament in 1970, Grant himself admitted that the situation
was not totally gloomy, citing the resurgence of nationalism
in the young. This resurgence continued throughout much
of the decade, and was especially evident in the arts
and among numerous academics and intellectuals. If the
Committee for Independent Canada became increasingly
inactive, this was at least partly because its ideas had

permeated many areas of society and sizable factions of all three political parties. Even the constitutional squabbles at the end of the decade could be regarded in a hopeful light. For all the pettiness they revealed, they also indicated a dogged determination on the part of many Canadians to reaffirm and redefine a distinctive Canadian nation.

At this point, I was becoming even less convinced by Grant's doleful prophecies, and I was starting to suspect that his logic was too compelling and his strictures too inclusive. As Hamlet told Horatio, there are more things in heaven and earth then any man's philosophy can envisage: despite the power of Grant's analysis, I wondered whether he was sufficiently aware of the sheer diversity of Canadian society, and the prickly reluctance of many Canadians to become mere ciphers in a universal homogeneity. As we have seen, Grant disdains the ivory tower. A public philosopher, he roots his ideas in "the wonder of lived experiences" and affirms the importance of "living in the world". And yet . . . his profession as a scholar and teacher may have induced a certain remoteness from the clamorous world which exists outside academia. I recall a warm summer afternoon when I took George and Sheila Grant to the races at Woodbine. After lunch at the Turf Club, I gave them an impromptu tour, ending up in the grandstand. All at once we were engulfed by stale smoke, by beer and mustard smells, by hundreds of patrons milling around the betting windows. Black, brown and white . . . men and women, some with children underfoot . . . a microcosm of the metropolis. "This is marvellous!" Grant thundered as he plunged into the crowd. "It's just what I needed! A moral philosopher must get out in the world!" This incident was decidedly endearing, and I would not make too much of it, but it does suggest that Grant is consciously if reluctantly remote from all the complexities of Canadian society. Sometime later, when Al Purdy was castigating "pompous intellectuals", I cited Grant as a delightful exception. Affectionately, if also incautiously, I went on to recount that Woodbine anecdote. Purdy leaned across the table, took my arm in a hard grip, and said with great emphasis: "Now that *is* pompous!" He paused, shook his head, and added scornfully: "Moral philosopher, indeed!"

It may turn out, of course, that Grant's prophecies will be ultimately fulfilled: by now, however, I was feeling less terminally pessimistic. It seemed to me that significant numbers of Canadians were concerned to remain distinctly Canadian, and that Grant may have overestimated the homogenizing power of liberal technology. Since I also suspected that many Canadians were equally determined to preserve their regional and racial identities—as a crucial part of the Canadian mix—I was far from convinced that an intelligent conservatism could not appeal to those adherents of diversity and particularity. Again, I could agree with Morton that a conservatism purged of all reactionary elements offered the only possible opposition to the statist, dehumanizing tendencies of liberal and social democratic thought. In short, I accepted that Grant had trenchantly identified the enemy, but I suspected that he had too readily conceded the outcome of the struggle.

Yet it didn't exactly help my inquiry that Grant himself had gone on—after *Lament*— from a preoccupation with Canadian issues to a much broader and equally pessimistic concentration on the fate of the whole Western world. After resolutely if regretfully affirming the impossibility of Canada's survival—and the impossibility of conservatism as a practical stance in our era—he had tended to immerse himself in much deeper philosophical questions. "What Trudeau is ... well that's not the most important matter compared to what God is." Grant told me, with a huge laugh, on one of my visits to Dundas. He added that he was only starting to get near to writing anything on really major themes. "What justice is—in the Platonic sense—I'd like to say something on *that* before I die."

Consistently, however, Grant has used contemporary issues as a springboard for his speculations. In the years after *Lament,* his fears about the basic inhumanity of Western liberalism were confirmed by the carnage in Vietnam. In an essay published in 1967—"Canada's Fate and Imperialism"— he maintained that Canada's involvement in the war went much deeper than its role of arms merchant and diplomatic ally to the Americans. Most Canadians had a basic belief in progress through technology, and that faith was identified with the power and leadership of the American empire:

> This then is why our present fate can be seen with such clarity in the glaring light of Vietnam. The very substance of our lives is bound up with the western empire and its destiny, just at a time when that empire uses increasingly ferocious means to maintain its hegemony. The earlier catastrophes and mass crimes of the age of progress could be interpreted as originating entirely with other peoples, the Germans, or the Russians. They could be seen as the perverse products of Western ideology—national socialism or communism. This can no longer be said. What is being done in Vietnam is being done by the English-speaking empire and in the name of liberal democracy.

Here we see that Grant's earlier lament for Canada was based on more than mere nostalgia for a vanished past. Nostalgia may have been the starting point: as he told a symposium on his work which was held at Erindale College in 1977: "Nothing so much can drive one to philosophy as being part of a class which is disappearing." But Grant sees Canada's fate in the context of Western man's evolution over the centuries; when he regrets Canada's adherence to "the rationalized kingdom of man", it is not from the narrow viewpoint of Victorian-Edwardian Toronto, but on the basis of moral philosophy from the time of Plato. When Grant laments the disappearance of indigenous traditions, including his own, it is because such traditions offer an approach to values and beliefs which have sustained other men in other cultures and other centuries. "It is true that no particularism can adequately incarnate the good," he states in "Canada's Fate and Imperialism". "But is it not also true that only through some particular roots, however partial, can human beings first grasp what is good and it is the juice of such roots which for most men sustain their partaking in a more universal good?"

It was this "universal good" which now preoccupied Grant, so much so that he seemed to have gone beyond even the highest level of red toryism to a position where all such political labels became inappropriate. In 1974, Grant indicated a new direction in his thought when he delivered a series of lectures at Mount Allison University which were later published under the title of *English-Speaking Justice*. By this time, he had long passed from thinking about the details of Canadian life to thinking about the nature of technological society and its implications for modern man. As we have also seen, he had long since abandoned any liberal faith in human progress. He had defined liberalism as "a set of beliefs which proceed from the central assumption that man's essence is his freedom and therefore that what chiefly concerns man in his life is to shape the world as we want it." As such, liberalism was linked with technology as part of that same dominant force which was leading to the universal and homogeneous state. In his Mount Allison lectures, however, Grant makes clear that there are some aspects of classical liberalism which he supports—like Morton he denies that conservatives need be anti-liberal. "Liberalism in its generic form is surely something that all decent men accept as good—'conservatives' included. In so far as the word 'liberalism' is used to describe the belief that political liberty is a central human good, it is difficult for me to consider as sane those who would deny that they are liberals." What now concerns Grant is whether traditional liberalism can survive in the universal and homogeneous state. Since technology is increasingly directed toward the mastery of human beings through such means as behaviour modification and genetic engineering, it may lead to oppressive political regimes which deny the liberal postulates of freedom and justice: "The practical question is whether a society in which technology must be orientated to cybernetics can maintain the institutions of free politics and the protection by law of the rights of the individual."

For Grant this dilemma is illustrated by a United States Supreme Court ruling that no state has the right to pass legislation which would prevent a citizen from receiving an abortion during the first six months of pregnancy. The Court affirmed the right of the mother to control her own body because it denied that foetuses were "persons in the whole sense". Grant notes that the ruling was greeted as an example of the nobility of liberal ideology, since the right of an individual was defended against the power of a legislative majority. But he warns: "If foetuses are not persons, why should not the state decide that a week old, a two year old, a seventy or eighty year old is not a person 'in the whole sense'? On what basis do we draw the line? Why are the retarded, the criminal or the mentally ill persons? What is it which divides adults from foetuses when the latter have only to cross the bridge of time to catch up with the former?" For Grant the ruling shows the dangerous inability of contemporary liberalism to sustain traditional concepts of justice against new claims on behalf of convenience. He concludes on a sombre note: " . . . it is improbable that the transcendence of justice over technology will be lived among English-speaking people."

If there is one word which *seems* to characterize George Grant's thought, that word is pessimism. His view of our fate has steadily darkened. From lamenting the disappearance of Canada in the American empire, he has gone on to describe how the imperatives of modernity are forcing all mankind toward a world order in which traditional concepts of justice, freedom and individual worth will be threatened by an awesome tyranny. From an early liberal faith that Western societies could further human excellence, he has passed through a red tory phase to a position which suggests that all democratic politics — liberal, socialist or conservative — are irrelevant in a world which is governed by technology and bureaucracy. Finally, he is even prepared to speculate that the entire Western experience has been some sort of gigantic error, with the implication that our brief interlude in the eternal order may be nearing its conclusion.

Sombre and gloomy, Grant's perceptions have brought him close to personal despair. He has described himself as an impotent stranger in the practical realm of his own society, forced to observe the "crazy chaos" of human existence in a world of "unspeakable evils and tragedies". His sense of loss goes much deeper than mere nostalgia for a vanished way of life, since it involves the erosion of moral values in which he finds the meaning of mankind. When Grant writes about "the battering of a lifetime of madness", we can sense the turmoil in his soul.

What is left for us, his readers, to make out of this? Logically, we should emerge from a study of Grant in a mood of gloom and desperation. If Grant is really unrelenting in his pessimism, if he regards his prophesies as bound to be fulfilled, then it is not only speculation about the future of Canada which is futile, since our whole world is doomed to darkness. In that case, any one of us might be excused for cynicism, for selfish hedonism. If political action is irrelevant, if philosophy leads only to despair, then to lose oneself in drink, drugs or sex might be the best of consolations.

And yet . . . this is not the message which I derive from Grant. Instead of gloom, somehow he induces hope. Again the paradox. For me, Grant is always exhilarating, despite his direst warnings. Judging by the growing number of younger writers and academics who wrestle with his writings, my reaction is far from singular. Now I was finally starting to understand the process. In predicting the worst, Grant also reminds us of the best—especially those classical standards of justice and freedom by which he judges our modern era and finds it wanting. He arouses not only our apprehension of man's propensities to evil, but also our awareness of man's timeless quest for the good. He seems to challenge us to prove him wrong.

This could well be his intention. For Grant is not so pessimistic as he often seems, nor is he advocating fatalism. Even his most sombre pronouncements are lightened by glimmerings of hope. He has speculated that an ultimate world tyranny is impossible, since men would break it down from boredom. More fundamentally, Grant thinks it is "the greatest of God's dispensations that no one can prophesy the future in detail." He has therefore explicitly ruled out cynicism and inaction as adequate responses to our situation. As he told a teach-in at the University of Toronto in 1965: "Nothing I said denies that justice is good, and that injustice is evil, and that it is required of human beings to know the difference between the two. To live with courage in the world is always better than retreat or disillusion." Courage is a high virtue for Grant, along with hope and love. Beyond those, "it is also possible to live in the ancient faith which asserts that changes in the world take place within an eternal order that is not affected by their taking place." It is finally impossible for Grant to be pessimistic, as he has said himself, since this would involve denying his vision of that eternal order. Implicit in all this is the hope—perhaps the conviction—that our current course can be reversed, and that the good will ultimately triumph.

Grant is carefully reticent about how this reversal might occur. He says it would be presumptuous for him to propose any particular therapy by which we might escape from the tight circle of the modern fate: "The decisions of western man over many centuries have made our world too ineluctably what it is for there to be any facile exit." But Grant lays particular stress on what he calls "intimations of deprival" — our sense of all that we have lost in our drive to conquer nature. He suggests that through philosophy and art, we can relive these buried memories of human excellence, and so retain some notion of the good. As William Christian has written: "Grant's conclusion is enigmatic. I take him to be uttering a prophesy which he hopes is self-defeating. He is, I believe, offering us a challenge to think together the achievements of modern science and of classical philosophy. Only if he can terrify us enough with the prospects of the impending darkness, will we see the need to struggle to remain in the light."

For me, that challenge seemed enough to get on with. It had also become the crux of my own reaction to Grant. In an imperfect world, we need such a trenchant moralist to arouse our apprehensions. Then, by our actions, we may yet avert or mitigate the disasters which he foretells, At the very least, I accepted as an imperative for any conservative the statement of Sir Thomas More which Grant has often quoted: "When you can't make the good happen, try to prevent the very worst."

Since I had received few glimmerings of an eternal order, I could not be certain that the good must ultimately prevail. But nothing in Grant made me believe that a universal tyranny was inevitable, or that modern technology had reached a point where it could no longer be controlled by concerned and thoughtful humans. If such was the case, then there was still room in the world for an independent Canada, and still room in Canada for an intelligent conservatism which could foster our particular traditions.

At this point, then, my own inquiry seemed far from futile. But it was beginning to appear one-sided. I had been dealing with conservatives who castigated the contemporary liberal alternative, even if they espoused much of classical liberalism. Perhaps I was stacking the deck, since it was all too easy to dismiss Canadian liberalism in terms of the baleful influence of Mackenzie King. While King's example was crucial and revealing, it hardly encompassed the whole of his tradition. In fairness, it now seemed prudent to explore the liberal alternative as seen in some of its more attractive avatars.

VII

Clear Grit:

Smith, Underhill, Galbraith and Trudeau

When Goldwin Smith settled in Toronto in 1871, he was already one of the most eminent liberals in the entire English-speaking world. He was forty-seven, and he had made his mark in both his native England and the United States. As an educator and reformer, Smith took a prominent part in all the great controversies of his day. Among his duties as Regius Professor of History at Oxford, he gave private lessons to the Prince of Wales; among his friends he numbered Cobden, Bright, Mill and Spencer, not to mention Prime Minister Gladstone. On one occasion, on a matter of protocol, even Queen Victoria followed his advice. During his first visit to the United States, in 1864, Smith conducted a triumphant lecture tour; he called on Emerson, Thoreau and Longfellow, and he was received by General Grant, Secretary of State Seward and President Lincoln.

This eminence derived largely from Smith's achievements as an incisive essayist and journalist. An archetypal
Victorian liberal, he attacked British imperialism and advocated colonial emancipation; with some reservations he also
supported *laissez-faire* economics, popular education and
social and labour reforms. An enemy of aristocratic privilege, and an enthusiast of American republicanism, he owed
his reputation in the United States to his unabashed support
of the North in the Civil War, at a time when the English
establishment was largely sympathetic to the South. Above
all, Smith had a passionate faith in freedom which won the
admiration of liberals on both sides of the Atlantic. Although
shy and reserved in person, he was ferociously indignant in
print, directing his scorn at political corruption, personal
cruelty and the obtuseness of his opponents.

It may be wondered why Smith chose to spend the last
half of his life in a city which, after Oxford and London,
struck him as a cultural backwater. In fact, although he was
to re-visit England frequently, he had already parted from
it, in 1868, to accept a professorship at the fledgling University of Cornell. His reasons for settling in North America
seem to have been complicated, and largely personal. Money
was not the object, since Smith was independently wealthy.
As both teacher and writer, he had an assured position in his
native country, where he also received several offers of
political preferment. It was a combination of events—
including the death by suicide of his father—which sent him
abroad; when he moved to Toronto three years later, it was
partly because he was distressed by the growing anti-British
feeling of many Americans (as a result of the Civil War and
the *Alabama* claims), and partly because he had cousins in
Toronto who could offer a refuge to the lonely bachelor.

As much as any of these, however, Smith had an abiding
faith in the prospects for "Anglo-Saxonry" and an equally
strong inclination to study the phenomenon in all its aspects.
By today's standards, the liberal Smith was equally a racist as

the conservative Leacock. (He was especially disdainful of Jews and Irish.) As much as any of the Canadian Imperialists who became his strongest opponents, he believed in the superiority of the Anglo-Saxon race. This qualifies his anti-imperialism; it is also a key to the continentalism which was his major contribution to Canadian political thought.

Although far from uncritical towards the United States, Smith regarded it as the greatest achievement of his race, and yearned for its reunion with the mother country. This would not be a political union: Smith was aware of the impracticality of such a goal, just as he was scathing about the vague notions of the Canadian Imperialists, and forever asking sharp questions about their precise proposals. To Smith, imperial federation was "simply one of the changes of hue on the dying dolphin of the old colonial system". Instead, he advocated a larger if looser union. Despite his doubts about the constituent parts—the American tendency to populist demagoguery, the corruption and factionalism of Canadian politics, the aristocratic chauvinism of the English—Smith believed that the Anglo-Saxon peoples were united in deeper values, especially their common attachment to the rule of law, to personal liberty and to freedom of opinion. Rather than a political federation, he espoused "a moral, diplomatic and commercial union of the whole English-speaking race throughout the world."

This cause became a crusade to which Smith devoted all his polemical skills. Initially, however, he did not favour continental union. For a time after his arrival in Toronto, Smith believed that the new nation might succeed as a second—and distinct—experiment in North American democracy: to this end, he advocated complete independence from Britain and lent his support to the young nationalists of the Canada First movement. Despite his convictions as a moderate free trader, Smith even voted for Macdonald and his National Policy in 1878 on the grounds that a temporary tariff was justified in such a young country.

But he soon became disillusioned with the quality of Canadian politics, in particular the jobbery and petty partisanship. When Canada First foundered after its leader, Edward Blake, was won back to Liberal ranks, Smith concluded that Canadians lacked the will to create a genuine nation. Even more crucially, he became convinced that Canada was an economic and geographic impossibility. Eventually, as Creighton noted, he was arguing against everything that Macdonald was espousing:

> Canada's continued membership in the British Empire, Smith considered, stunted the growth of a genuine Canadian national feeling; the persistent solidarity of French Canada hindered the development of a national unity; and, perhaps most important of all, the geography of North America divided Canada into a series of regions, more closely connected with similar regions in the United States than with themselves. The American and Canadian economies, in Smith's view, were complementary, not competitive; he had not the slightest doubt that the idea of founding a separate Canadian nation on an east-west axis was a huge mistake. With greater force, cogency, and wit than anybody else, he set out the fundamental antithesis to Macdonald's thesis of the Canadian nation.

These views were trenchently argued in *Canada and the Canadian Question* which Smith published in 1891. As he now saw it, Canada had been created only out of "sentiment" and the new nation was bound to succumb to the "primary forces" of geography, commerce and the shared identity of race, language and institutions. In fact, he claimed, Canada was already an "American community" and an integral part of a larger liberal and democratic society; it was now necessary only to sweep away such feudal remnants as the

monarchy and to seek formal political and economic integration with the United States. In this way, Smith concluded,
Canada could attain "the glorious era of perfect order and
civilization".

In future decades, such views became commonplace
among continentalists: Smith's book is still the classic case
for North American union, and it anticipates all those
inexorable pressures of liberal technology which Grant was
later to lament. At the time, however, Smith was widely
reviled for such unpopular and unpatriotic arguments.
Canada and the Canadian Question came out during the 1891
campaign—an election which Macdonald won on the basis of
loyalty to "The Old Man, the Old Flag, and the Old Policy",
and because the voters suspected that the Liberals' enthusiasm for reciprocity contained an unstated yearning for
eventual political union. In the aftermath of the election,
Smith was called a traitor by some of Macdonald's more
fervent supporters. That most intemperate of the Imperialists, Col. George Denison, stated publicly that Smith should
be in jail.

On the grounds of free speech, many of Smith's opponents rallied to his support. Despite his views, moreover, he
was always an influential member of Canadian political and
intellectual circles. In 1875, he had married Harriet Boul-
ton, the widow of a former mayor of Toronto. Their home,
The Grange, was one of the oldest and most splendid in the
city; here Smith entertained an unending procession of both
Canadian and foreign dignitaries. (Noting the way in which
he handed his butler the keys to the wine cellar, the young
Vincent Massey was impressed by Smith's adherence to
social ritual.) Wealthy by inheritance, and aristocratic by
temperament, Smith was liberal not only in his writings: he
gave generously of his money—and his time—to a host of
civic charities. To the new nation he also brought the best
traditions of English nineteenth-century journalism, which
was then at its peak of erudite commentary. As a frequent

contributor to Canadian magazines and newspapers—and
sometimes as their financial backer—he did much to raise
the intellectual level of Canadian political discourse.

Despite these attractive aspects—and despite the fact
that Smith remained a Torontonian until his death in
1910—there is a sense in which he never came to terms with
his new home. Disraeli once called him "a wild man of the
cloister", neatly suggesting both Smith's state of perpetual
indignation, and his remoteness from the world outside his
study. As his biographer notes: "His study was his arsenal,
and the periodicals of England, Canada and the United
States his field of battle. This had its unfortunate side. He
was too much a man of letters to move freely among
ordinary people. His own philosophic belief in eternal
principles and in the rationality of man made him singu-
larly ignorant about human nature."

This also has its attractive side. Smith's curiosity was
insatiable, and his cosmopolitan interest in all the great
contemporary issues was a welcome antidote to the parochial
nature of most Canadian political and social debate. But it
suggests why his repeated assertions that Canada's destiny
lay in union with the United States received—for all their
impeccable logic—such a lukewarm response. According to
Principal Grant, Smith simply did not understand the
deepest feelings of ordinary Canadians: he never grasped
that breaking with Britain and joining with the United
States would involve a disruption of associations and traditions which few Canadians were willing to contemplate. To
Smith, such feelings were merely "sentiment"; to Grant, they
embodied some of the strongest impulses in our national
life.

Confident in his liberalism and his cosmopolitanism,
Smith was certain that rational self-interest would ultimately
prevail over those tiresome regional and patriotic loyalties.
He was contemptuous, not only of Canadian politics, but
also of the diversities they revealed. He supported continen-

tal union partly because it would hasten the demise of all such particular traditions, especially the stubbornly unassimilated conservatism of Quebec. Here again, Smith foreshadowed the later Grant in recognizing the homogenizing power of American liberalism: "Nationalities are not so easily ground down in a small community as they are when they are thrown into the hopper of the mighty American mill."

In a letter which he wrote in 1893, Smith said that the height of his ambition would be fulfilled if he could die in Canada an American citizen, with England's blessing on the arrangement. Since he was already seventy, he added, this was unlikely to happen. In fact, when Smith finally died, well into his eighties, it was one year before the 1911 election in which Canadians again defeated a Liberal party pledged to reciprocity with the United States. But the cause which Smith had espoused so fervently did not die with him. If later generations of Canadian liberals were less open in their continentalism, they were often just as dogged in working for closer political and economic links with the United States. In retrospect, it seems appropriate that the Laurier government's official delegate to Smith's funeral was its young Minister of Labour, W. L. Mackenzie King.

Among the ushers at Goldwin Smith's funeral was an undergraduate at the University of Toronto who had been recruited for the occasion. Again in retrospect, this, too, was appropriate. For the undergraduate was Frank H. Underhill and he was to become not only an eminent historian, but also an iconoclast and polemicist who increasingly viewed Canada's destiny in terms of the larger North American community. If Smith was the most distinguished prophet of continentalism, Underhill was to prove one of his most influential acolytes.

This was the result of a gradual process: Underhill was a youthful socialist who accepted the desirability of an independent Canada, and who emerged only in his later years as an unabashed supporter of the Liberal party and an advocate of closer links with the United States. To a limited extent, his political evolution parallels that of Eugene Forsey; to a much greater degree, Underhill resembles Smith in his tendency to see Canada in American terms — and to find it wanting.

Born in 1889, Underhill came from English stock and was the son of a boot maker and local politician in the village of Stouffville, near Toronto. As William Kilbourn has noted, it is difficult to think of a man whose life style and very being — as well as thinking and writing — would stand in sharper contrast to that of Donald Creighton, his near contemporary and fierce rival. Underhill's family was Liberal in politics and Presbyterian in religion; according to Kilbourn, it was logical that a Clear Grit from that North York farm country which supplied the Mackenzie rebellion with its best recruits should become the chief gadfly of the Family Compact's spiritual descendents.

Always conscious of his lower-middle class origins, Underhill seems to have been inherently skeptical and puritanical in his responses to the socially more sophisticated contemporaries he encountered at the University of Toronto (where he studied classics, English and history from 1907 to 1911), and at Oxford's Balliol College, to which he subsequently won a scholarship. His incipient radicalism was fed by Oxford tutors who were among the leading Fabians of their day; it was confirmed by his experiences during World War One, when he served as a subaltern officer in an English infantry battalion. Underhill would always speak approvingly of British intellectual traditions, but the war convinced him that Canada's future lay outside the British orbit. As he later wrote: "The stupidity of G.H.Q. and the terrible sacrifice of so many of the best men among my contemporaries sickened me for good of a society, national or international, run by the British governing classes."

Underhill had spent the first year of the war as a professor of history in the University of Saskatchewan. Returning to his post in 1919, he was swept up in the agrarian protest movement which was challenging the basic structures of Canadian politics. Later he would describe the gatherings of angry wheat growers as the greatest revival meetings ever held in Canada: "I exulted in the refusal of the prairie farmers to be fitted into the old two-party system of eastern Canada, or into the orthodox religious denominations of Ontario—the United Church was born on the prairie—or into the dominant banking and financial system of Montreal and Toronto."

In 1927, Underhill joined the history department of the University of Toronto; he also became a regular book reviewer and columnist for the *Canadian Forum*. By now he was thoroughly engrossed by Canadian politics; like Smith, he became one of the most incisive essayists of his day. (Although he would write scores of scholarly articles, he never produced a full-length book.) As the Depression took hold, Underhill became outspoken in his attacks on the capitalist system. With fellow academics from Toronto and Montreal, he founded the League of Social Reconstruction; then, in 1933, he helped to write the Regina Manifesto which heralded the birth of Canada's first social democratic party, the CCF.

In his socialist period, Underhill was a long way from Goldwin Smith's brand of early Victorian liberalism. Like Smith, however, he started as a nationalist who became increasingly skeptical about Canada's ability to maintain a separate destiny in North America—and increasingly scathing about the level of Canadian political, social and cultural life. In an essay on Smith which he published in 1933, Underhill echoed his mentor's basic criticism: "The gristle of our frame has never matured and hardened into bone." Throughout the next three decades, he continued to describe Canada as a cultural and political wasteland. There was no other country in the world, he maintained, in which intellectuals were held in such low repute. A placid and lethargic people, Canadians were incapable of tragedy, and smugly remote from all the great upheavals of the twentieth century. As a result, our politics remained "mean, drab, petty, insignificant".

Much of this was the polished invective of a master polemicist: Underhill always delighted in offending the self-righteous, including his more soporific colleagues. But much of it was also based on his conviction that political and intellectual life was much more interesting in Britain and (especially) the United States. Above all, Underhill castigated Canada for its lack of a strong radical tradition: "If we search back into our history, we find that the reason for this is that the first great liberal democratic upheaval in nineteenth-century Canada, the movement of Papineau in Lower Canada and of Mackenzie in Upper Canada, the movement which was our Canadian version of Jacksonian democracy, was a failure." Increasingly, Underhill came to view Canadian politics as an insipid and immature variant of the stirring activities which occurred within the great republic, contrasting in particular the dynamic Roosevelt with the plodding Mackenzie King. Increasingly, too, he came to attack earlier Canadian historians like W. P. M. Kennedy and Chester Martin for emphasizing the conservative and British traditions in Canadian life. To Underhill, these were not nearly so crucial as the fact that Canadians and Americans were linked in a common endeavour— creating new political societies while developing a new continent—and that, in many ways, "the United States is simply Canada writ large."

This, of course, was the doctrine which soon became orthodox and which Creighton would describe as the Authorized Version of Canadian history. It led Underhill to maintain that Canadians should turn away from their European ties and seek to achieve the liberal values which animated the United States. Unlike Goldwin Smith, he never stated specifically that full political and economic union with the United States was either inevitable or desirable. But from the start of World War Two—and especially with the outbreak of the Cold War—he argued that Canada had no choice but to become a loyal ally of the Americans in all their global ventures.

In the autumn of 1940—after the fall of France and the signing of the Ogdensburg Agreement which set up a permanent joint board for North American defence—Underhill gave a controversial talk at the annual Couchiching Conference. Speaking without a text, he held that Canada's destiny would increasingly depend upon continental co-operation—whatever the outcome of the war. As he was reported as saying: "We now have two loyalties—one to Britain and the other to North America. I venture to say it is the second, North America, that is going to be supreme now. The relative significance of Britain is going to sink, no matter what happens."

Like Smith, Underhill was attacked as a virtual traitor by much of the Toronto establishment; not for the first time, there were demands that he be dismissed from his university post. With the help of academic colleagues (including Creighton) and high-placed Liberal friends in Ottawa, Underhill weathered the crisis. While he became more discreet in his public utterances, however, his views remained unchanged. They also received increasing approbation. With the outbreak of the Korean War, Underhill became convinced that the United States was leading a great crusade to preserve the world for liberal democracy, and that it deserved the fullest Canadian support. This was the view of the Ottawa mandarins, the view which so appalled Innis and Creighton. While Underhill accepted that the Americans were still uncertain in their diplomacy—and could benefit from loyal Canadian advice—he held that the test of Canadian maturity lay in how sensibly Canadians adjusted to the new phenomenon of American leadership: "Mature people accept the inevitable."

In the nineteen-fifties, and increasingly thereafter, many Canadians who were otherwise mature began to worry about the threats to Canadian independence which were posed by the overwhelming influence of the United States. Underhill dismissed their concerns as "storms of neurotic emotion" and was especially patronizing to those who feared the total Americanization of our popular culture. To Underhill, the phenomena of American movies, American radio and television, American magazines and American advertising were just "typical expressions of a society in which the masses have at last arrived and are demonstrating their lack of interest in the more severe intellectual and moral standards of an older aristocratic civilization." As always, he was condescending about Canada's failure to achieve its own revolution of mass democracy: "But we all have to go through it in our turn; and turning our backs on the United States will not save us. We have no native inherent sense of higher standards which might preserve our Canadian purity if we could shut out the American invasion." When the Massey Report was published in 1951, Underhill scorned its advocacy of a culture which would be independent of American influences: "It is too late now for a Canadian cultural nationalism to develop in the kind of medieval isolation in which English or French nationalism was nurtured. The so-called 'alien' American influences are not alien at all; they are just the natural forces that operate on a continental scale in the conditions of our twentieth-century civilization."

It seems an inevitable result of such thinking that Underhill by this time was shifting his political allegience from the CCF to the Liberals. According to Creighton, Underhill had never been deeply engaged by the CCF's social and economic theories: "His real aim was North American continental unity; and, under the foreign policies of King, St. Laurent and Pearson, this aim was coming closer and closer to realization." In *Lament for a Nation* George Grant studied Underhill's conversion from his own point of view, noting how the former opponent of big business could announce, in a 1964 speech, that the liberal hope lay with the great corporations: "Professor F. H. Underhill is a key figure in the intellectual history of Canadian liberalism . . . . . He has recognized that the business community in America is no longer the propertied classes of his youth but managers whose ideology is liberal. He is right to believe that corporations and not doctrinaire socialism are the wave of the future."

Underhill's conversion was underlined in 1960, when he dedicated his collected essays to Lester Pearson. By then he had left the university and accepted Pearson's invitation to become curator of Laurier House in Ottawa. Long the home of Mackenzie King, and stuffed with his possessions, Laurier House was a shrine to both King and the Liberal party. By then, too, the conversion was complete. Sometime after Underhill's death in 1971, his former adversary described with typical Creightonian scorn "the apotheosis of Underhill as a great spiritual leader of twentieth century Canadian Liberalism":

> [It] came with the dinner which celebrated his eightieth birthday. It was held in the Rideau Club in Ottawa and was very much a Liberal establishment affair. There must have been well over a hundred diners. A few old associates in the founding of the CCF were there: but the later leaders of the party, and of its successor, the NDP, were conspicuous by their absence. Most of the academics present came from the two faithful strongholds of Liberal thought, Queen's and Carleton University; and there were several representatives of the federal civil service, that unofficial but powerful arm of the Liberal party. These were the intellectuals who had helped to build the one-party Canadian state, whose convictions, loyalties and antipathies had taken concrete shape in the reality

of modern Canada. They were aging now, but they had finished their work and were well satisfied with it. Their former leader, L. B. ("Mike") Pearson, who had done so much to realize Underhill's continentalist foreign policy, appropriately made the first of the laudatory speeches; and Underhill responded with a bland air of conscious political virtue and acknowledged political success. "I simply cannot understand the view prevalent today," he declared to his delighted audience, "that there is something vicious about the Liberal establishment." The happy diners laughed their agreement. They were established, secure, and complacently comfortable in the prospect of the indefinite prolongation of Liberal rule.

As proclaimed by Smith, and embraced by Underhill, continentalism became one of the strongest impulses in Canadian liberalism, and in the policies of the Liberal party. Initially this impulse sprang from a determination to throw off the remnants of British rule. Increasingly it was fed by the liberal tendency to give priority to economic factors and to see Canada as part of a vast North American industrial empire. From King through Trudeau, Liberal leaders have flirted from time to time with nationalistic policies, but these have been temporary aberrations, and it has often taken only a bark of disapproval from Washington to cause their curtailment, if not their abandonment.

There is more to this than servility. If Canadian liberalism has difficulty in articulating any clear sense of nationhood, it is not only through fears of American retaliation. While such fears are often crucial, liberals have deeper reasons for resisting a nationalist stance. As Christian and Campbell have argued, nationalism or patriotism is based on an appreciation of history and tradition, as well as a sense of a collective entity which is superior in some respects to its individual members. To a liberal, these are dubious values, and Canadian liberals in particular have found it difficult to perceive any clear differences from their co-ideologists to the south: "Preoccupied with escaping British ties they were blind to the new bonds they were forging. The liberal commitment to individual liberty made them loath in the extreme to place restrictions on it for collective, nationalist ends."

For me, a commitment to individual liberty was an obvious imperative. If our democratic rights could be strengthened and extended through continental union, then I would find it hard not to forsake my nationalism and to join the liberal ranks, even the Liberal party. But Morton had convinced me that freedom, justice and human diversity could flourish best within the context of an intelligent conservatism, and I had come to share Grant's apprehension that these same values were increasingly menaced by the liberal technology of which the United States is the greatest progenitor. Again, I had to concede that Canadians were usually less assiduous than Americans in asserting their individual rights, and that this was a negative result of our conservative emphasis on peace, order and good government. But I agreed with Grant that liberalism, with its commitment to technological progress, was creating the conditions in which all such rights would be imperilled within a universal and homogeneous state. The closer our ties with the liberal republic, therefore, the less chance there would be to retain not only our distinctive conservative tradition, but also the freedom and diversity which that tradition was armed to protect. In short, it seemed to me that Smith and Underhill were not so much prophets of our emancipation, as unwitting exponents of our ultimate enslavement.

These two great liberals shared another trait which I also came to challenge, although with somewhat less conviction. As we have seen, they viewed Canada as a political and cultural backwater. To both, our public affairs, our intellectual life and our artistic creativity were distinctly second-rate. At least until recently, there was much truth in this, and even George Grant could identify certain advantages to our assimilation in the larger American empire: "We leave the narrow provincialism and our backwoods culture; we enter the excitement of the United States where all the great things are being done. Who would compare the science, the art, the politics, the entertainment of our petty world to the over-flowing achievements of New York, Washington, Chicago and San Francisco? Think of William Faulkner and then think of Morley Callaghan. Think of the Kennedys and the Rockefellers and then think of Pearson and E. P. Taylor." One suspects a certain irony here, but it is hard to counter the assertion that we *have* been inferior—and often derivatively so—in all these aspects. True, the last two decades have seen a surge of creativity, and a growing appreciation that Canadians have a distinctive culture of their own. Yet it is possible that future generations may be less than effusive in their praise of our contemporary artists, writers and musicians; certainly their present reception often smacks of self-congratulation. In our determination to assert a national identity, we too often hail the merely mediocre. Such smugness is the bane of nationalism: just as conservatives can become stultified in their social awareness, so nationalists are prone to be parochial. In this respect, both Smith and Underhill did some service: by invoking the highest intellectual standards of their time, they challenged our complacency.

Both, in short, were cosmopolitans. But if this had its attractive side, it was also patronizing and dismissive. To Smith and Underhill, Canada was incomplete and immature because it clung to a stubborn conservatism which was manifest among both English and French Canadians. With their liberal belief in rationality and self-interest, they were impatient with the non-liberal aspects of Canadian life, especially the tory touch which they condemned as stifling, undemocratic and—especially in North American terms—decidedly anachronistic. As Gad Horowitz has written: "The secret dream of the Canadian liberal is the removal of English Canada's 'imperfections'—in other words, the total assimilation of English Canada into the larger North American culture." This dream is still at the heart of Canadian liberalism: in different ways it permeates the careers of two of liberalism's most distinguished contemporaries, John Kenneth Galbraith and Pierre Elliott Trudeau.

I met John Kenneth Galbraith in the spring of 1977, when he came to Toronto to promote his $2-million television series, *The Age of Uncertainty.* For the purpose of a magazine article, I tracked the famous economist's giant, gaunt frame as Galbraith endured—with unshakable courtesy and professional aplomb—a series of radio and television interviews, a press conference, a literary luncheon and a book-signing in a department store. Enormously tall at six feet, eight and a half inches, Galbraith moves with the awkward lope of a man in constant apprehension of upsetting the furniture. His drab suits hang loosely from his lanky frame. His face, a slab of craggy mountainside, conforms to his own description (in his book, *The Scotch*) of his boyhood neighbours in southwestern Ontario: "They were made to last. Their faces and hands were covered not with a pink or white film but a heavy red parchment designed to give protection in extremes of climate for a lifetime. It had the appearance of leather, and appearances were not deceptive. This excellent material was stretched over a firm bony structure on which the nose, often retaining its axe-marks, was by all odds the most prominent feature."

Instantly recognizable, Galbraith was greeted everywhere as a celebrity, and it occurred to me that few Canadians had such a towering international reputation. Among intellectuals, Northrop Frye and the late Marshall McLuhan were the two other names which came to mind. But Frye and McLuhan lived and worked in Toronto: to many Canadians this would suggest that both had failed to make the big time. Galbraith, on the other hand, had spent four decades mingling with the movers and shakers in Washington and New York, London and New Delhi, Moscow and Peking: this international acceptance was an essential ingredient of his undoubted glamour. During World War Two, he had gone from Harvard to Washington to direct Roosevelt's program of price controls. Later he became a stalwart in the liberal wing of the Democratic party, an advisor and speech writer to the likes of Adlai Stevenson, the three Kennedys, Lyndon Johnson, Hubert Humphrey, Eugene McCarthy and George McGovern. ("I have had a growing affinity for lost causes," he says, in a mock attempt to disparage his reputation as a power behind the scenes.) Galbraith had been an editor of *Fortune* and was still a professor at Harvard; along the way he had worked in a stint as John F. Kennedy's ambassador to India. His memoirs are studded with personal impressions of the great, from Henry Luce to Henry Kissinger, Jawaharlal Nehru to Jackie O. Above all, Galbraith has made his name as a writer. Since *The Affluent Society* was published in 1958 and stayed on the best-seller lists for thirty weeks, a dozen or so of his books have sold literally millions of copies around the world. Thanks to mass-market paperbacks and his flair for conveying a dusty discipline in provocative aphorisms, Galbraith has become a household name among the educated.

In all these roles, Galbraith has emerged as one of the most formidable of modern liberals. In support of liberal causes, he has long been lavish with his time and his talents. One of his books—published in 1960—was dedicated simply to "The Blacks", and Galbraith was one of the earliest opponents of the Vietnam War. When I met him in Toronto, he had just been granted access—under the Freedom of Information Act—to the Galbraith dossier which the Federal Bureau of Investigation had been compiling over the previous three decades. "It's several inches thick and it took several days to read," Galbraith told me proudly.

Above all, Galbraith has spoken out against the tyranny of big corporations and big unions. Like Grant, he argues that technology has made inevitable the increasing centralization and sophistication of power. But Galbraith accepts this phenomenon as a challenge which a rational mankind can yet harness to its own democratic ends. Specifically, he holds that it is up to governments to control the corporations and the unions, and thus ensure that the affluent society will benefit all its members. To many of his critics, however, this stance has taken Galbraith beyond liberalism to a dangerous advocacy of highly centralized and paternalistic regimes. According to Simon Reisman, the former deputy minister of finance and archetypal Ottawa mandarin, Galbraith is a revolutionary who could demolish the supporting pillars of neo-classical economics, including consumer demand, the free market and open competition. "All his reform measures have a common ingredient: a large and ever growing role for the state," Reisman has written. "He would reduce the emphasis on economic growth, shift massively from private goods to public services, redistribute income towards an egalitarian society and introduce permanent wage and price controls to regulate large corporations and unions . . . . . In a sense he substitutes the dictatorship of the intelligentsia for the Marxian dictatorship of the proletariat."

Far from abashed by such attacks, Galbraith strenuously defended his theories during his Toronto trip. To interviewer after interviewer, he maintained that large corporations and large unions had rendered obsolete the traditional economics of the market place. Governments, he said, must protect their citizens through wage and price controls, since these were the only alternative to runaway inflation and massive unemployment. Although Galbraith claims he is not an advocate of big government for its own sake, he regards its further growth as inevitable.

There was an extra edge to the questions of Galbraith's interlocutors, since his views had provided the underpinning for several of Prime Minister Trudeau's speeches on wage and price controls—a policy with which the Liberal government was then experimenting. In a television interview, Trudeau had acknowledged the economist's influence: "I'm not as wise and experienced as Galbraith," Trudeau said, "but there's no doubt that his thinking has permeated my thoughts and that of a lot of other people."

To many outraged Canadian tories, this simply confirmed the obvious: that Trudeau was a socialist, if not actually a communist. In fact, of course, both the liberal and the conservative traditions in Canada have long made a place for measures which are loosely labelled socialist, including a significant amount of government activity to restrain private greed and protect the disadvantaged. Any red tory is bound to echo Galbraith's criticism of big business and big labour; any red tory is certainly no automatic opponent of controls and social welfare. What bothered me about Galbraith, however, was the *extent* of his prescriptions, and especially his calm acceptance of an ever-growing government bureaucracy. Such a bureaucracy could only imperil those traditional liberal values—notably freedom and diversity—which it has become the task of conservatives to protect. As always, however, Galbraith had a quick rejoinder: "The people against big government are those who need it least. Criticisms of the welfare state don't come from those who depend on it." Fair enough—there is no doubt that Galbraith's intentions are compassionate. But I couldn't help regarding this humane and decent man as—even more than Smith and Underhill—an unwitting prophet of Leviathan.

Listening to Galbraith was strangely akin to reading Grant. In their very different ways—the one with cheerful complacency, the other with moral outrage—both have acknowledged that the power of liberal technology is almost unlimited in our era, and that it is leading to an increasingly homogeneous world order. For Grant, the loss of his indigenous traditions is part of this process, and one of its most lamentable aspects: "It is true that no particularism can adequately incarnate the good. But is it not also true that only through some particular roots, however partial, can human beings first grasp what is good and it is the juice of such roots which for most men sustain their partaking in a more universal good?"

As with Grant, so with Leacock, Creighton, Morton, Forsey and Purdy. Each has cherished his particular roots. With Galbraith, on the other hand—and this now seemed a key—there is no such passion, no such "juice". When Morton recalled his youthful toilings behind a plough, it was with pride in the rituals of pioneer life, and a strong feeling for the land. In his memoirs, Galbraith is typically sardonic about a similar background: "A long day following a plodding, increasingly reluctant team behind a harrow endlessly back and forth over the uninspiring Ontario terrain persuaded me that all other work was easy." True, one of his finest books, *The Scotch*, is an affectionate account of his origins in the small farming community of Iona Station. But Galbraith makes clear that the ties were always tenuous: "We were taught that Canadian patriotism should not withstand more than a $5-a-month wage differential. Anything more than that and you went to Detroit."

For Galbraith, it wasn't Detroit, but the University of California and then on to Harvard and Washington, where he was one of those enthusiastic young professors who set about reforming the American economic system under FDR. All this was accomplished without the slightest qualm. According to Galbraith, the Scottish Canadians of Elgin County "were, of all the peoples of the world, the most nearly emancipated from the burdens of national passion.

Our school books featured the Union Jack as the front, spoke warmly of Major General James Wolfe, William Lyon Mackenzie, Louis Joseph Papineau, Sir John Alexander Macdonald and King George V. But none of these stood against the better hours, more congenial work and vastly higher pay in the United States." In 1937 Galbraith became an American citizen — "the least traumatic action I ever took."

Here I was struck by the contrast between Galbraith and Leacock — two Ontario farm boys who made good, and achieved international eminence. When Leacock was touring the British Empire and giving lectures on imperial unity, he wrote letters to his family which expressed a strong desire to establish roots on his return. When he finally built his home on Old Brewery Bay, near Orillia, it was a celebration of those roots and traditions: an Ontario summer home in the grand Edwardian manner, with just a touch of Gallic panache. Galbraith, the ultimate cosmopolitan, has a home in Cambridge, Massachusetts, a farm house in Vermont and an apartment in Switzerland.

Like Smith and Underhill before him, Galbraith regards Canadian patriotism as an anachronistic sentiment. To him, "the burdens of national passion" are just that: a barrier to the workings of rational self-interest. True, Galbraith told me that Canadians might usefully concentrate on developing greater autonomy in such fields as television, book publishing and education. But he implied that such efforts might well be doomed to ultimate failure. Modern industrial states have increasingly uniform social and cultural preoccupations, no matter who controls their institutions. In the case of Canada, he added, our proximity to the United States could only accelerate the drive to homogenity.

With his rational liberalism, Galbraith seemed out of touch with popular feelings in his native land, including the widespread revulsion against the burden of federal government spending and the powers of the Ottawa bureaucracy. He was unsympathetic to provincial viewpoints and said flatly that Canada would not break up, since no people ever takes drastic action against its own economic self-interest. In this case, I hoped that he was right, but it did occur to me that here again, Galbraith's cosmopolitan liberalism made it difficult for him to comprehend the diversity and strength of our regional and racial aspirations.

Yet Galbraith has never really escaped his origins. His father was a sometime teacher and a Liberal organizer who is credited with the dubious distinction of bringing Mitch Hepburn into politics. His forebears, like those of nearly all his neighbours, were Scots Highlanders. As Galbraith describes them, the Calvinist inhabitants of Elgin County were practical and dour (except when fighting drunk), anti-English, anti-tory and highly suspicious of all appeals to King and Country. As such, they were "the predictable mass, the solid rank and file of the Liberal Party". In his memoirs, Galbraith acknowledges a life-long debt to this background:

> In Upper Canada (now Ontario) in the last century . . . there was a moral and political cleavage between the rural Scotch and the prestigious Toryism of the English-oriented ruling class. The resulting attitudes were far from dead in my youth; they required that one be compulsively against any self-satisfied elite. One never joined, and one never overlooked any righteous opportunity to oppose or, if opportunity presented, to infuriate. No psychic disorder could be more useful. It forces one automatically to question the most pompously exchanged cliches of the corporate executives, the most confidently vacuous voices on military adventures and the most generally admired triteness on foreign policy. To me it has been valuable, I believe, on matters as diverse as the deeply sanctioned obsolescence of neoclassical economics and the greatly self-approving commitment in Vietnam.

As often with Galbraith, I find it hard to read that passage without an approving chuckle. The role of the liberal iconoclast is attractive and necessary, and few have filled it with such distinction. Like Smith and Underhill, Galbraith has been a staunch opponent of the "conventional wisdom" (his own phrase). As the enemy of cant and hypocrisy, as well as sheer stupidity (Vietnam), he has given notable service, while adding to the general merriment. And yet . . . something in that passage also rankles. The scourge of self-satisfaction shows more than a trace of it himself. Sir Francis Bond Head and Professor Milton Friedman are easy targets . . . neither the Family Compact nor modern neo-conservative economics have much to do with thoughtful toryism in any part of North America, and certainly not with the conservative tradition which I have been exploring in this book. Above all, it is the dry intellectualism which bothers me . . . lots of wit, but no juice. When Galbraith writes—in the very first sentence of his memoirs—that "The southern Ontario countryside is devoid of topographic, ethnic or historical interest", he is being deliberately provocative. But there is something demeaning and diminished in such an attitude . . . ultimately we are being patronized.

Perhaps it isn't *only* patronizing. Galbraith dwells on his roots to an extent which suggests that he really takes some pride in them, if only the secret pride of any Scot for his scraggy, ancestral braes. But if he feels a baffled nostalgia for his background, Galbraith leaves us in no doubt that such feelings have never been transformed into the burdens of national passion. His cosmopolitan flair is much more crucial, and it is this which makes Galbraith an archetypal Canadian liberal. For all his charm and compassion, he finally emerges as an enemy of human particularity . . . and as the consummate continentalist. As Galbraith's close friend, Walter Gordon, has remarked: "He's an American now; he sees things from the standpoint of the American Empire." To recall Horowitz: "The secret dream of the Canadian liberal is the removal of English Canada's 'imperfections'—in other words, the total assimilation of English Canada into the larger North American culture." For such liberals, Galbraith is their apotheosis—the Ontario farm boy who rose to the dizzy heights of Harvard and Washington, and who looks back on his origins only with querulous amusement.

Let us watch him at his moment of triumph—the culmination of his political career. It is a brisk April morning and Queen Elizabeth II has just taken off from Ottawa, leaving behind an ornate, hand-lettered parchment which she and her Canadian First Minister have duly signed. Back on the tarmac that same First Minister, insouciant as ever, and with the inevitable red rose in his lapel, is exhausted but also exhilarant. As the cameras click and whirl, Pierre Elliott Trudeau essays a modest pirouette.

True, his triumph is flawed. It hardly mattered when *The Globe and Mail* harrumphed that although any number of politicians are adept at fancy footwork, "... most of them have a keener sense of timing, a better sense of humour and a sounder sense of place." For it is likely only a handful of Canadians was offended by Trudeau's *lèse-majesté* and many more would grant that he had cause to celebrate the patriation of Canada's new constitution. But it *did* matter that after months of bickering and acrimony, there was more relief than rejoicing in the land. The deed was finally done, but the costs were still to be counted. Both the federal Liberals and several provincial premiers were skeptical about the compromises which each had forced upon the other: both the Quebec government and the native peoples were protesting that their rights had been betrayed. Whatever else ensued, it was certain that many a legal and political battle would be fought before the constitution became an effective reality. When Trudeau made his pirouette, it looked less like a victory dance than a flourish of his customary bravado.

Let us grant him this—when he presided over the patriation of that new constitution in the spring of 1982, Trudeau completed the grand task which had brought him into federal politics nearly seventeen years earlier, and into which he had dragged—at times almost willy-nilly—the entire Canadian nation. This task was not so much the severing of Canada's last remaining links with Britain (barring our shared monarchy): these ties had long ceased to have any practical import, and not even the staunchest anglophile could realistically resent their abandonment. More crucially, Trudeau had established a federal framework which aspired to protect the basic rights of all Canadians, and to give French Canadians in particular a plausible alternative to the dubious benefits of separation.

This goal has often seemed the one fixed element in a career which enshrines the volte-face as the supreme political manoeuvre. Trudeau has long shown his contempt for the electorate: his flip-flops on major policies (wage and price controls, foreign ownership, oil prices, etc.) exceed any of his exploits from the high board. During the fourteen years that he has led the Liberal party, the Grits have become a coterie of cynical opportunists: not even Mackenzie King was more blatant in his lust for office.

As with his career, so with his character. There are so many paradoxes and contradictions to Trudeau that he almost defies rational analysis. The carefree bachelor who married a pathetic flower child and then won wide sympathy for his dignified transition to single parenthood. The advocate of "participatory democracy" who lost all faith in the people and referred to their elected representatives as "nobodies". The stalwart war leader of the October Crisis ("Just watch me!") who smeared his reputation as a champion of civil liberties. The advocate of reason over passion who has argued so passionately for a civilized, bilingual nation. The world statesman whose policies are so devoid of practical substance. The ruthless political infighter who delights in crushing his enemies, but who still conveys the impression he would be happier on some university campus. The icy intellectual who (in Richard Gwyn's felicitous phrase) often appears in the guise of a "*farouche* Peter Pan".

Through all these contradictions, however, Trudeau eventually emerges not as some exotic aberration in our political history, but as a conventional liberal in the tradition of Smith and Underhill, King and Pearson. His politics are firmly based on the classical liberalism of Mill and Locke: from his early writings as an anti-Duplessis activist, to his pronouncements as Prime Minister, Trudeau has stressed the absolute value of the individual, and the supremacy of reason over emotion. As one of his biographers, George Radwanski, has noted: "Although freedom is the highest value in Trudeau's system, it is not the ultimate objective. The real goal is individual self-perfection, and Trudeau has the classical liberal's belief in the infinite perfectability of man. He accordingly defines ideal freedom in its broadest sense, to mean the absence of all obstacles — physical, material or cultural — to a self-fulfilment whose precise nature each person must decide for himself."

This individualism underlies Trudeau's well-known hostility to all forms of nationalism, whether Quebecois or Canadian. He denies that the state has any collective purpose which is greater than its individual members: "Men do not exist for states; states are created to make it easier for men to attain some of their common objectives." As rhetoric, this is heady stuff; in reality, however, men and women *do* have disconcerting loyalties to their racial grouping and their geographical roots. This does not imply the fanaticism of a Hitlerite Germany or the bellicosity of a Reaganite America: Trudeau has clearly failed to appreciate Orwell's distinction between nationalism — which is based on the aggressive drive for power — and patriotism, which is defensive, and based on devotion to a particular place and particular way of life. In turn, this explains in part why Trudeau is often so abrasively unsympathetic to the particular loyalties and aspirations of individual Canadians — whether they be Newfoundlanders, Quebeckers or Albertans. As with Galbraith, one feels a lack of "juice". This is the fatal flaw of the cosmopolitan. As George Grant has said: "I know that most people who are cosmopolitan lack something essential. That is why I distrust Trudeau so greatly . . . . . You feel in him a real dislike for ordinary French Canadian life, and even a dislike of the deeper roots which made French Canada distinct. Whatever Lévesque's mistakes, one does not feel that superior cosmopolitanism in him. One feels a love of his own in all its rough particularity."

Trudeau's liberal individualism is also the key to one of his apparent paradoxes. Baffled by his shifting policies, at times both his opponents and his disappointed admirers have concluded that he is fundamentally conservative, or else a raging red. But this was never quite the point. As Richard Gwyn has written: "Democracy, civil liberties, rationalism. For Trudeau, these were the essentials. Once they were achieved, the particular political system that a particular state adopted mattered incomparably less." In turn, this explains the theory of "counterweights" and his belief in "functional politics". Always the pragmatist, Trudeau has sought an appropriate balance between the major contending forces — whether these be Ottawa and the provinces, business and labour, free enterprise and state intervention. Through all the twisting and turning, he has sought to protect — and if possible expand — the areas of individual freedom.

Again, this is admirable in theory. In practice, however, it has led Trudeau *away* from democracy and classical liberalism, and towards those technocratic politics which Grant has described as the greatest threat to traditional concepts of freedom and justice. With his belief in rational planning, Trudeau has created a governmental and personal bureaucracy from which ordinary Canadians have come to feel increasingly remote. According to James and Robert Laxer, Trudeau sees political leadership as an exercise in social engineering: "Very much in the mould of intellectual liberalism with its realist posture, he regards the passions and desires of the people as a highly dangerous force that must be contained and directed to keep the ship of state on its proper course." Contemptuous of grass root feelings—just because they *are* feelings—Trudeau believes that an elite of cool technocrats, gathered at the centre, is best suited to develop policies which can then be presented to the people as a rational consensus of what is best for them.

Even in pragmatic terms, this approach has clearly failed. Perhaps our economic problems are largely insoluble; far from containing them, however, Trudeau and his technocrats have given us record levels of inflation, unemployment, government spending and national debt. Although bilingualism may be counted a partial success, the way it was imposed has proved divisive: again, Trudeau showed himself insensitive to the fears and aspirations of ordinary Canadians. Although we have our new constitution, it is a better document than Trudeau tried to impose on us, mainly because the federal Conservatives and a majority of provincial premiers refused to submit to Trudeau's timetable. Worst of all, it is no longer possible to take Trudeau seriously as an advocate of human freedom. During his tenure, our national police force has become an instrument of political repression, our civil liberties have been eroded, the civil service has been debased through blatant patronage, and parliament and the cabinet have been downgraded in favour of elitist managers. Like Galbraith, Trudeau appears committed to an ultimate dictatorship of the intelligentsia.

In all this, Trudeau the democrat has been subsumed by Trudeau the technocrat. As further proof of his decline, consider his remarks on the imposition of martial law which shut down Polish freedom. For a year and a half, Canadians had watched with admiration as the members and supporters of Solidarity struggled with courage and audacity to alleviate the burdens of their Communist tyranny. But when Solidarity was quashed, and its leaders imprisoned, the Canadian Prime Minister could conclude only that martial law was preferable to the shooting and starvation which he had come to regard as the inevitable result of Solidarity's "excessive" demands. As always, Trudeau was realistic in his response. (Remember "Where's Biafra?") But as Robert Fulford has pointed out, Solidarity's "excessive" demands involved only the basic rights which Western trade unions had enjoyed for most of this century, and which the earlier Trudeau would have recognized as just and reasonable: "His remarks on Poland, which have alarmed and shamed so many of us, demonstrate what has happened to his attitudes during his time in government. Like many a politician and bureaucrat before him, he has moved over to the side of power, whatever form it takes."

At this point, Trudeau's much-touted realism becomes little more than cynicism. In the pursuit and exercise of power, Trudeau has divided us as never before, bribed us with our own money, and taught us that honesty and civility are for losers. As a result we have mortgaged not only our economic future, but also our self-respect. Trudeau's legacy to Canada is an increment in sleaziness, an alarming growth in our *psychic* national debt.

By now I was convinced that Canadian liberalism had largely failed us. From Goldwin Smith to Pierre Trudeau, it has often championed the cause of human freedom and individual excellence. By the late twentieth century, however, its vision of Canada was terminally bankrupt, and its democratic rhetoric was patently fraudulent. Because they are cosmopolitans who disdain all those particular loyalties which give deeper meaning to our lives, liberals are incapable of articulating any sense of shared nationhood. Because they are social engineers who are bewitched (for all their prideful rationality) by the powers of technology, they are ultimately compelled toward conformity and authoritarian arrogance. Increasingly our liberals are obsessed with their own rectitude, and ruthless in their lust for power. When they conjoin in the Liberal party, they become one of the worst of all human groupings — a conspiracy of cynics.

By now, too, I had concluded that there was still room in Canada for an intelligent conservatism which could foster our independence and provide ample scope for the human rights and the human diversity which are part of our joint heritage. In exploring the conservative tradition, I had discovered aspects which seemed formidably relevant to our present situation, and which might commend themselves to other Canadians. Somehow I couldn't accept that everything was lost. This was partly a matter of faith, for which I make no apology. It was also largely theoretical, which was almost certainly a drawback. I had immersed myself in books and — even more — in conversations with a small group of thinkers and writers. They were a diverse lot, with different outlooks and roots in different regions, but they were hardly a cross section of anything, except the conservative temperament. It was never my intention to draw up a specific political program, or to meddle in the bloody vendettas which so exercise the Progressive Conservative party, but I began to feel that it was time to get away from theory for a while, and to test my optimistic instinct in more practical realms. It was even time to talk to politicians.

VIII

Tradition and Renewal:
Stanfield, Crombie and the Future

In all the years I toiled as a journalist—roughly my twenties and thirties—I rarely covered any aspect of Canadian politics. By choice and good luck, I had made the world my beat: at different times I was more familiar with the pecking order in the Chinese politburo or tribal tensions in Zimbabwe than I was with the issues and intrigues which engaged my colleagues in the Parliamentary Press Gallery. On occasional forays to Ottawa, I observed its leading denizens with minimal enthusiasm: only the early Trudeau seemed any sort of match—in intellect and style—for the likes of Chou En-lai or Julius Nyerere. Based in London during the Diefenbaker years, I was embarrassed whenever the Chief stormed windily into town; in time I also came to regard Lester Pearson's good-guy diplomacy as little more than a stalking horse for Washington's global ventures. In short, I was hardly inspired by our leaders, whatever their political persuasion.

Soon after I launched this exploration of the tory
tradition, Joe Clark came to power at the head of a minority
Conservative government. At first this seemed a happy
omen: my ignorance of Clark was almost total, but he was
clearly decent and honest, and his advent was a sharp rebuke
to the Liberal hucksters. Perhaps — one dared to hope — there
was still some life in the once-dominant Conservative tradition, now to be redefined by a young man from the burgeoning West. Had I shared the experience and cynicism of my
Press Gallery colleagues, I might have known better. At any
rate, those early hopes were quickly dashed. Petrocan and
"privatization" . . . it all seemed mindless and at times fanat-
ical, the fruits of an ideological passion which derived more
from Margaret Thatcher and Ronald Reagan than Sir John
A. Macdonald. (Point to recall: real conservatives are *never*
idealogues.) Soon the Conservatives appeared as the pup-
pets of Bay Street and the blue-eyed sheikhs. If the ideology
was misguided, the incompetence was calamitous: out-
manoeuvered and finally outvoted by the Grits, the Conservatives returned to their familiar places on the opposition
benches, and to their familiar pastime of knifing each other
in the back. Himself was restored as our Perpetual Leader,
and the smiles on the faces of Keith Davey and Jim Coutts
raised smugness to the realm of the sublime.

Small wonder that I steered well clear of Ottawa in my
early peregrinations. Small wonder that my only trips to our
National Capital Area (typical Grit term) were to meet
Eugene Forsey. Given the political ineptitude and intellectual confusion within the Conservative party, it seemed that
the real guardians of the tory tradition were to be found
among the academics and the artists. Eventually, however, I
changed my mind. Eventually I came to believe that the
conservative tradition did have some life in it — some
considerable life — and that many Canadians were searching
for an alternative to the tarnished liberal dream. If there was
any hope for conservative ideals, it was to the politicians,

especially those in the Conservative party, that one must look for their implementation. Given the sorry record and ignominious defeat of the Clark government, the prospects of a tory revival seemed highly tenuous. Over the years, however, I had met a few Conservatives—Flora MacDonald, David Macdonald, David Crombie—who were my kind of tories. Along the way, I'd heard of a few others such as Douglas Roche and Gordon Fairweather who seemed to fit the bill. And there was one Conservative, whom I had never met, who had striven long and hard to heal the wounds of the Diefenbaker era, to reaffirm the basic tradition, and to give his party's platform a hard edge of contemporary relevance. Three times rejected by the voters. Perhaps the Best Prime Minister We Never Had. In retirement now, and scrupulously avoiding any involvement in his party's inter-necine struggles. But watching . . . watching everything from his Rockcliffe home . . . with time to reflect and ponder. Too big a man to overlook. And so I went to see Robert Stanfield.

When you drive to Rockcliffe Park from downtown Ottawa, you go along Sussex Drive, past three obvious landmarks. First comes the Lester Pearson Building, a neo-Aztec pile which is totally devoid of grace or distinction. (The newish home of External Affairs, it is a near perfect visual correla-tive of the bureaucratic mentality, exceeded only by that more recent horror, the massive government complex across the river in Hull.) Then there is blessed relief—the comfort-able, unassuming grey stone residence of the Prime Minis-ter which is soon followed by the simple yet elegant gateway and winding parkland drive to Rideau Hall, home of the representative of the Crown in Canada. In both cases, the security is minimal— an RCMP sedan in the entrance of the PM's home; two sentries, resplendent in their scarlet tunics and black busbies, at the gate of Rideau Hall. Strung with cameras, a few tourists stroll casually in front of both places—unhurried and unhassled. Here, at the symbolic heart of Canada, on a sparkling summer afternoon, I have a welcome sense of peace, order and good government—as well as a dignity and a hierarchy which are mercifully free of bombast. Here, at least, our traditions still make sense.

Stanfield lives with his wife in an unpretentious white stucco house with a bright yellow door. He answered the bell himself, dressed casually in brown slacks, a brown-and-white T-shirt and brown oxfords. A lugubrious countenance, with just a hint of incipient humour. (Later I found a perfect description of Stanfield on a similar occasion: "The door opens, and I'm confronted with the face of a woeful but friendly beagle, half-hidden smile and a courteous nod to enter . . . . . His big knurled hands, like a fisherman's, that sculpted and improbable head, something out of Stonehenge.") Somewhat apologetically—explaining that passing buses made conversation difficult in the living room—he led me to the back porch. He'd been sitting there with a book on trees, contemplating the leafy ravine and sorting out the different varieties.

Some weeks earlier, as a prelude to our interview, Stanfield had sent me a small collection of his writings. Nothing bulky or pretentious—just a few papers which he hoped would give me some idea of his concerns. I already knew how he had sought to revamp the Conservative party in the wake of the Diefenbaker debacle, partly by attracting bright new MPs, partly by trying to convince Quebeckers that the Conservatives were more than just a party of *les anglais,* partly by establishing a Policy Advisory Committee (under Trent University's Tom Symons) which produced a plethora of new ideas. All this, of course, had been to little immediate avail. On three occasions—1968, 1972 and 1974—Quebec held solidly to the Liberals and enough voters in the rest of the nation were sufficiently enthralled with Trudeau to keep the Grits in power. According to popular judgment, the former Nova Scotian Premier was an honourable man, but much too bumbling for our television era. And when he dropped that football.....But as Jeffrey Simpson wrote, if Stanfield could never match Trudeau's public allure, he "at least made the Conservative Party a more modern institution than it had been under Diefenbaker, receptive to fresh ideas and more interested than before in future problems than past battles." In particular, he had tried to demolish the image of the tories as the party of the smug and well-to-do. The party should be recognized, he had said, "not merely for its affluence, for its comfort, for its power — but for its humanity, for its compassion, and for its decency."

All this was confirmed by one of the papers Stanfield sent to me. It was the text of a memorandum to the members of his caucus in November, 1974: the swan-song of a three-time loser who knew that his power was ebbing, but who was determined that his party should not slip back into reactionary ways. Tactfully but firmly (the tone is that of a long-suffering schoolmaster lecturing an habitually wayward class), Stanfield argues that the true conservative is neither a doctrinaire supporter of private enterprise nor a diehard opponent of necessary reforms. While conservatives had always favoured a limited role for government — "I think it is fair to say that the Conservative statesmen we respect most were innovators" — in the tradition of Macdonald they were never afraid to use the power of the state for the national good, and they did not place private enterprise on a pedestal. While conservatives stressed the importance of order, this meant not merely "law and order" but also social order. In turn, this implied concern for the poor and disadvantaged, concern for the environment and concern for the effects of economic growth: "I suggest that it is in the Conservative tradition to expand the concept of order and give it fully contemporary meaning.... Resistance to change and the support of privilege has been part of the behaviour of Conservatives from time to time, but neither is nor ought to be Conservative principle."

Reading all this, I was reminded of what Tom Symons had told me: "For seven years I saw or spoke to Mr. Stanfield nearly every day. During all that time he never had a crummy thought. He moved the party forward with his concern for the fabric of society and for society as an organic entity. Don't forget—he comes from a disadvantaged part of the country. Perhaps that's why he had such sympathy for the different regions, and for the aspirations of the farmers, fishermen and workers. He was a genuine reform tory. He reminded the party of its heritage."

Yes, indeed. Stanfield stood for the conservative tradition at its best. And yet . . . he'd never made it to 24 Sussex Drive. I also wondered whether Stanfield had, in fact, revitalized his own party. Whether his ideas had really taken hold in that caucus of notorious intractability. There was the brief record of his successor's government—hardly a triumph of progressive toryism. And there was the more recent evidence that the electorate still saw the Conservative party as the narrow and reactionary voice of privileged groups. Just weeks before my trip to Ottawa, the pollster Allan Gregg had told a party strategy session that when people think tory they think old, narrow-minded, cranky, slow, not with it, not chic, not successful, not competent and not for women, the working man or minorities. Not surprisingly, Gregg concluded that this image of the party was a "prescription for disaster" at the polls.

So now I was asking Stanfield—had he really made much impact on his party? Had he really opened it up to fresh ideas? Stanfield considered the question carefully. It could hardly have taken him by surprise, but his manner—here and throughout the interview—was slow and deliberate. There were long pauses, hard thinking and a sense of intensity which was occasionally relieved by sudden chuckles. "I always thought I was in a minority in the party," he finally answered. "Of course," he added with a wry smile, "most people who call themselves Conservatives don't necessarily have a philosophy at all." I suggested that the present caucus had few tories of his inclination. Stanfield nodded his agreement. "The present caucus reflects Conservative strength in the West. Rugged individualism and simplistic social views are rather common there. It will take a little time for that to change."

All this was very balanced, very philosophical. There was no bitterness or spleen in Stanfield. No digs or easy jibes. Even his references to Diefenbaker and Trudeau (he called them both "Mr.") were scrupulously fair. By now I was starting to feel a bit uneasy. I admired Stanfield's dignity but was bothered by his lack of passion. I didn't always expect the explosive vehemence of a Creighton or a Grant, but I did like my tories to have a certain flair. It seemed to go with the territory.

Soon, however, Stanfield was speaking with greater feeling. I reminded him of his strong reaction to Trudeau's scheme to patriate the constitution without the approval of the provinces (this was before the final compromise of November, 1981): Stanfield had called it "a constitutional *coup d'etat*". "Yes I *do* feel strongly," Stanfield said. "Mr. Trudeau violated the federal nature of this country. Whatever happens we'll have bitterness and bitchiness for years." As with the constitution, so with oil policies—here, too Stanfield showed an instinctive sympathy for regional sensitivities, and a deep puzzlement over Trudeau's motives. "I think I understand a great deal of what he's done over the years, but I don't understand any of this." Again he stared at the trees for several long moments. "Do we proceed by confrontation or consensus? Mr. Trudeau has chosen confrontation. I keep asking myself—can this possibly work? I don't think so. Is he really uniting the country? Obviously not. I think some degree of reconciliation is urgent!" Stanfield went on to say that it wasn't a question of giving more power to the provinces: this was neither necessary nor desirable, and he thought that Joe Clark agreed with him.

"It's more a question of how the existing powers are used. The federal government has to be the great regulator." Again he stressed the need for consensus rather than con-. frontation. Suddenly he added, with a laugh: "But then I've never tried to run the country!"

But I wasn't there to delve into specific policies. Instead I wanted to test my growing hope that some form of intelligent, compassionate conservatism might still be relevant to Canada. So I asked Stanfield—did he share George Grant's pessimism? Now he became even more pensive. Now the pauses were even longer. "So many things *are* disturbing," he finally said. "The means of manipulation are so prevalent . . . . . You wonder how much principles are going to count . . . . . Television seems to form most people's attitudes . . . . . During elections, there's no real discussion, just media events . . . . . There *are* lots of reasons to be pessimistic."

Chin on hand, Stanfield seemed absorbed in watching a flight of birds. Then he turned back to me, "You know," he mused, "I'm not so certain that *everything* is getting worse. There's less confidence in the natural evolution of progress than there was a few years back. Instead of everyone doing their own thing, there's more feeling about the importance of society as a whole." Somewhat tentatively, Stanfield cited the environmental movement as one of the forces which were helping to foster a new sense of community. "It should be possible to have a conservatism which is based on some sense of order and community. I can't quite see that technology should make that impossible. To gain strength, the Conservatives need a few simple principles which the public can support. The Conservatives could win if they could create an impression that the party's basic concern was about the quality of society. Most people seem to be asking—is the consumer society the be-all and end-all?" Then he added, quickly and drily, "Of course, it's all right for *me* to ask that, sittingly comfortably in Rockcliffe..."

Stanfield went on to say that he respected Grant, and liked him. But he suggested that theorists and academics often overlooked the complexity of society. "Take economists, for instance. They've never been able to explain how things really work, or how they could be made to work. People can be swept off their feet by impressive theories ... but a conservative has so little confidence in theories." He gave a huge laugh and looked quite pleased with himself. "Perhaps *that's* my best answer to George Grant!"

Now it was time to leave. Later it would occur to me that Stanfield had taken me back into some of the territory that Morton had opened up. Both had viewed Grant's pessimism as a valuable starting point. The prairie historian had gone further than the Maritime politician in urging a complete acceptance of unqualified pessimism, in order finally to purge one's intellectual system of any rationalist assumption of inevitable progress. But both would agree that a compassionate conservatism—non-ideological and non-teleological—offered the best guarantees for freedom and diversity, and the best opposition to the conformist, dehumanizing tendencies of the liberal technological state. Although deeply troubled at the state of the country (and clearly not too happy about the state of the Conservative party), Stanfield saw some signs that the tide might be turning.

These were the views of an experienced politician, but I had to acknowledge that Stanfield was no longer practicing his profession. Suddenly I had a disturbing image of my tory thinkers more or less marooned in their separate eyries. I thought of Morton in Winnipeg, Creighton in Brooklin, Grant in Dundas and now Halifax ... each with friends and followers, but each also giving the impression of holding down some lonely outpost. In that sense, a home in Rockcliffe could be just as isolated as a tower in Academe. What I needed now was some further confirmation that these conservative ideals and values were still cherished—and still being *used*—in the cut and thrust of day-to-day politics. Again, I had some idea of where to look.

It was in the spring of 1978 that I first saw David Crombie in action. The place was Whitney School in the north end of Toronto's Rosedale riding. It was also the first time that Crombie and Dr. John Evans had appeared together for a political debate. A federal by-election had been called in Rosedale, and the Conservatives had nominated Crombie, who was just completing his third term as one of the most popular mayors in Toronto's history. Evans, his Liberal opponent, was a political novice with a brilliant record as a medical doctor and university president: for several months, the Grit hierarchy had been touting him as a rising star. It was clear that the victor would take a prominent place on his party's front bench: from the start, the race in Rosedale was billed as a battle between future Prime Ministers.

I had already interviewed both candidates—for the purpose of another magazine article—and had developed a clear prejudice against John Evans. This had nothing to do with his personality, which was attractive, nor with his public record, which was admirable. What rankled was the manner of his entry into politics. More than a year earlier, Davey and Coutts had seized on Evans as a promising star candidate to revive the party's fortunes in Southern Ontario and provide new lustre to the Liberal front bench. There then ensued a careful buildup, most of it at the taxpayers' expense. Evans accompanied Trudeau to Washington for a meeting with President Carter (he kissed Elizabeth Taylor's hand), and was later named to the National Unity Task Force, touring the country and gaining even more exposure. The final accolade had come when Trudeau made a surprise appearance at Evans' nomination meeting—the ultimate laying-on of hands.

I attended that meeting. More than 4,000 people crammed into the ballroom of the giant Sheraton Centre: most were presumably voting delegates, but they seemed outnumbered by the armed guards, the television cameramen, the marshals with walkie-talkies, the cabinet ministers and the hordes of Establishment figures and media celebrities. (*"Le tout Toronto* is here," a prominent Liberal academic giggled in my ear.) To the embarrassment of the party hierarchy the nomination was contested: they had failed to secure a graceful withdrawal from Anne Cools, a young black community worker who had some standing in Rosedale. When she had her chance at the microphone, Cools gave a hard-hitting speech in which she urged the Liberal party to "vigorously reform and cleanse itself". Judging by the perfunctory applause, this was not what *le tout Toronto* had come to hear. When his turn came, Evans was articulate, plausible and totally unmoving. Handsome, lean and clean-cut, he looked the part, but his speech was dull and platitudinous. Yet the outcome was never in doubt: Trudeau had not come all the way from Ottawa to anoint Anne Cools.

All this, of course, was typical Grit opportunism. Our Permanent Governing Party has long been adept at co-opting dissident tories, dissident socialists and those—like Evans—who had no apparent affiliation but who might well garner a multitude of uncommitted votes. When their usefulness was ended, they would receive the inevitable payoff: a seat in the Senate or a lucrative post on some government board. With Evans, it was generally held that Davey and Coutts must have dangled an even more intriguing possibility: a clear run at the top job when Trudeau gave it up. In this case, however, the Liberals had made one fatal error: they matched Evans, still relatively unknown, against the enormously popular Crombie. This was never their intention, since Crombie was expected to run in nearby Eglinton, and only accepted the Rosedale nomination late in the day.

From the start, it was hardly any contest, even though Rosedale had not gone Conservative since the Diefenbaker era. On that evening at Whitney School, Evans was again polished and articulate. When he talked about the economy and national unity, he sounded patently sincere. But much of the time he looked strained and even bored; he also seemed to patronize his audience. It was all very dry, without warmth or feeling.

Crombie was less glib, and held his audience much better. He had a way of bouncing on his feet, and using his arms and hands: it drew us to him, and made us feel involved. Even the sloppiness of his diction—the way he slurred the ends of words—worked to his advantage: in comparison, Evans sounded too precise and even prissy. Crombie's boyish charm was very much on display. It was easy to see why the columnists had dubbed him our Tiny Perfect Mayor, "as resistible as a puppy" and "a tiny little muffin of a man". Crombie is only 5' 5", and I sensed that many of the comfortable matrons in the audience felt a distinct desire to mother him. Yet I was also struck by Crombie's authority—it was evident when he attacked the Liberals for their misman-agement of the economy, but it was even more apparent when he spoke about his sense of Canada. Quietly, but strongly, he talked about travelling across the country, evoking the actual landscape for us. He spoke of three instincts which were held by all Canadians: a common belief in the land itself, a passionate regional identification, and a tenacious faith in our national traditions. But Canadians were starting to lose their grip, he warned. "Where has all the promise gone?" he asked with rising emphasis. "This country needs to quicken its blood . . . . . This country needs to turn itself around . . . . . *We need to dream again!*"

When Crombie sat down, the applause was loud and warm—much more fulsome than it had been for Evans. Still, the Mayor was on friendly territory—this was the sort of middle-class neighbourhood he had fought to preserve from the developers—and I couldn't tell how deeply the audience had been moved. Somewhat to my surprise, however, *I* was stirred by Crombie's rhetoric. It was folksy and down-to-earth, yet soaring and idealistic. But it also troubled me in a way that I didn't immediately comprehend. Later, I realized that Crombie had reminded me of Diefenbaker. ("I see a new

Canada," Diefenbaker proclaimed in 1958, on the eve of his sweeping election victory, "...a Canada of the North!") Well now, here were grounds for reflection. At his best—in those first two glorious campaigns—Diefenbaker had evoked a pride and optimism which had long lain dormant in us, a sense of our Canadian community and our Canadian landscape which not even Trudeau at his most eloquent had since been able to incite. Once in power, however, the Chief had let us down too badly and too often: it made one skeptical of electioneering visions. At this point, then, my feelings about Crombie were very mixed. But if he was striking a similar chord to Diefenbaker, it was probably a hopeful sign that his manner was less grandiose.

There was another difference: if Diefenbaker often seemed to operate on raw instinct, Crombie had a highly developed sense of his own ideological evolution. When I visited the Mayor in his City Hall office, he spoke of growing up (in the Toronto suburb of Swansea) in a home that was solidly CCF: both his father and grandfather were trade unionists. But he broke with this background when the CCF joined the Canadian Labour Congress to form the NDP. "The marriage of trade unions and a political party is a European, not a Canadian or North American phenomenon," he told me. "The NDP was interested in power. To the CCF, power was always secondary. So the moral difference was dissipated." Crombie said he respected Diefenbaker for his populism, and was greatly influenced by *Lament for a Nation*. But it was his experience as a city dweller in the nineteen-sixties which brought out his basic conservatism.

By then Crombie was teaching political science at Ryerson Polytechnic Institute, including a course in urban affairs. Newly married, he was also starting to raise a family in a tree-lined, middle-class neighbourhood in north Toronto. According to legend (which Crombie says is only partly true), he ran for City Council in 1964 because a developer had announced plans to put up a high-rise in the area. Crombie was defeated, but soon found himself allied with other budding politicians who also sought to halt the runaway development which was destroying neighbourhoods and turning Toronto into a concrete wasteland. It was an idea whose time had come. Elected as an alderman in 1969, Crombie startled the pundits three years later by winning the mayorality over two old guard candidates. Only 36, he found himself leading a reform council which set out to change the face of Toronto.

Mainly they succeeded. The legacies of the Crombie era were a city housing authority and a Central Area plan: both were concerned with keeping Toronto as a place where people could live. In essence the plan said that downtown Toronto must be more than rows of monumental office towers: there had to be housing, shops, parks and theatres to keep the place alive at night. To achieve these goals, Crombie mediated between the radicals and the die-hards on City Council, often taking his initiatives from the left and using the right as a brake. A strong debator and a skillful negotiator, he seemed to thrive on late meetings and last-minute crises. In time some of the radicals would charge that Crombie was never a serious reformer, that he adopted half-measures which were superficially attractive but which failed to alter fundamentally the rules of development, housing and transportation. But Crombie never pretended to be set on uprooting the whole system: he always regarded the "urban revolt" as a conservative movement. As Val Sears has written: "He made a middle-class city for middle-class people. And by harnessing the political force of neighbour-hood activists, he contrived to make working-class neigh-bourhoods better places to live as well." The radicals might jibe, but this was what the people wanted. Basking in the world-wide press coverge of Toronto as a humane and civilized city, Crombie was returned to office with massive majorities in 1974 and 1976.

Reviewing these years with Crombie, I sensed that the Mayor was a tory populist with a visceral link to the voters. Informality and openness had been the marks of his regime: the Toronto phone book carried his address and phone number under "Crombie, Mayor David", and he told me that he received about 150 calls a week from strangers — people with blocked drains, people needing ambulances and drunks from the Sapphire Tavern wanting Anne Murray's phone number. Most of the time, Crombie bubbles with humour. Always quick with a quip, he even manages to turn his lack of physical stature to advantage. "You know," he likes to say, "I'm the tallest Crombie in 75 years. When I go to family reunions, I just *lurch* around." For all the humour and boyishness, however, Crombie had authority and confidence, and there was also a hint of something sombre, at times a sadness in the eyes.

It was another three years before I saw Crombie again. As expected, he trounced Evans by a two-to-one margin. (Peering over a battery of microphones on election night, Crombie chortled: "You know what? We're really thumping them!") In the general election the following winter, he defeated Anne Cools by an even larger spread. Appointed minister of national health and welfare in the new Clark government, Crombie soon became alarmed at the reactionary trend in both the cabinet and the caucus. Already, in his maiden speech, he had reaffirmed his own populist bias, arguing for a more humane and flexible system of social welfare. Borrowing a phrase from Disraeli, he said that Canada was still "two nations" — one of the haves, the other of the have-nots. To be a have or have-not was not only an economic condition, he added, "it is in fact a condition which is moral, psychological, and indeed spiritual."

In the subsequent months, Crombie survived both a heart attack and the Conservative defeat. (In the 1980 election, he again held Rosedale easily.) Increasingly, he became a Conservative spokesman in the great debate which was launched by Trudeau's plan to patriate the constitution in the face of opposition from most of the provinces, Here, again, he was able to talk about our strong regional loyalties, our feeling for the land, and our attachment to our traditions. But this was not dry, academic chaff: Crombie sprinkled his speeches with references not only to Innis, Creighton and Farthing, but also to Gilles Vigneault, Monique Leyrac, Gordon Lightfoot and Stompin' Tom Connors. While not opposed to patriation, he warned that our feelings and traditions must not be sacrificed in the process: the British North America Act was "not just a piece of paper that you chuck away". Similarly, our basic rights did not come from governments (as the Liberals were asserting): instead, rights were meant to *limit* governments. Quite explicitly, Crombie was attacking the liberal impulse towards homogeniety and statism, while proclaiming a conservative belief in human diversity. Above all, he echoed Stanfield in defending the Canadian instinct to deal with differences through consensus: "Tolerance, civility and compromise, those are the tools Canadians used, not the drawing of lines, not compulsion and not unilaterally."

At the same time, Crombie was becoming more outspoken in opposing his own party's drift to the right. In talks with journalists, he said the Conservatives were going against their best traditions with their determination to "privatize" crown corporations and to introduce regressive social legislation. Too many of his caucus colleagues were obsessed with the American fad of neo-conservatism: "We've got to forget this nonsense of chasing every civil servant out of town." From afar, it seemed that he had launched an uphill battle, but Crombie himself was cheerfully maintaining that the party could be turned around, and that his vision of conservatism could pay off at the polls. "After all," he said, "Canadians live with liberal rhetoric, but we conduct our lives as social conservatives." For me, in the midst of my research, that rang a lot of bells. It was time to see Crombie again.

On a sunny morning in late spring, I met Crombie at the ferry docks in Toronto Harbour. As he came towards me—bustling and almost bouncing—he looked leaner and fitter than he had during that first Rosedale campaign. In a light brown suit, white shirt and darker brown tie, Crombie seemed overdressed for the occasion, but it turned out that he was later to open a new hospital wing. The trip to Centre Island had been his idea. "I like to get away from my desk," he explained, but with my inherent suspicion of politicians, I couldn't help thinking that it might have been contrived to show him at his best. If so, it worked—both on the ferry and along the Island paths, Crombie was constantly recognized and often warmly greeted. As he chatted to ticket-takers, maintenance men, school children and picnickers, I felt my cynicism ebb away. This was more than contrivance: Crombie was on his own turf, mingling with his people. It seemed to feed him.

For an hour or so we strolled under the trees and stopped to have a hot dog lunch. Our conversation lacked coherence. If Stanfield's speech is painfully slow and deliberate, Crombie's sentences keep tumbling out and running off in all directions. By coincidence he had also been researching a book on the conservative tradition, but was doubtful he would ever get it written. ("Writing really tears my guts. That's OK if you're a real writer—then it's part of the territory. When it happens to a non-writer like me, it's hell.") As we ranged from Leacock to Grant, it struck me that Crombie was neither a profound nor an original thinker. (In this, he reminded me of myself.) Rather he was something of an intellectual squirrel, gathering ideas, storing them in his mind, and chattering away about them with enthusiasm and excitement. I found this exhilarating. For just about the first time since I started my research, I even found myself relaxing. I had enjoyed losing myself in the flow of Forsey's anecdotes; but for all their charm and courtesy, many of the other tories had been overwhelming in their intellectual authority. Creighton's passion and Morton's calm wisdom were equally intimidating, while a conversation with Grant is like being attacked by a renegade steam roller—one is finally pulverized. In different ways, Purdy's gruffness and Stanfield's dignity had also kept me on edge. With his engaging effervescence, only Crombie really put me at my ease.

This is part of his populism. When Crombie talks about "ordinary people"—as he often does—it comes across with not a trace of condescension. Take, for example, his thoughts on Canadian nationalism. Contrary to many scholars and journalists, Crombie feels that Canadians are as patriotic as they've ever been, even if they seldom show it. "Our vision of Canada has been obscured by decades of American cultural intrusion, and our march to materialism. Beneath all that, though, the hearts kept beating. Right now, we're going through yet another empire. First it was the French, then the British, now the Americans. We're not out of it yet. We're still muting our Canadianism. But it's there. Canadians instinctively feel they're better than Americans. When I go around the country, I can see it in their eyes. I *feel* it!"

Like Morton and Purdy, Crombie roots his vision in the land: to him this is an essential part of the patriotic impulse. "Canadians regard the land as their birthright. It doesn't matter whether they're farming in the Okanagan Valley or living in a Toronto high-rise. Maybe it's not something they talk about very much. When I speak to Canadians about the land they're kind of uncomfortable. It's as if I'd spoken to them about loving each other. But the feelings are there."

In all this, of course, Crombie was the direct opposite of those liberal cosmopolitans who are always so patronizing about our feelings for our roots. For a moment I thought of

Grant, and his appreciation of Lévesque's "rough particular-ity". More and more, however, Crombie was reminding me of Morton: in their different ways, the Toronto politician and the Manitoban historian were both speaking to that same prideful sense of place. Then it struck me—Crombie was the plain man's Morton. For me, Morton's liberalism had provided an intellectual bridge to the conservative tradition, and made it seem distinctly relevant. Now I was beginning to sense that a populist like Crombie might well bring that tradition to the hustings, and make some impact. All at once, my optimism seemed more than merely theoretical.

Yet I still had doubts. I told Crombie that I wasn't so sure about all those apartment-dwellers. And what about new Canadians? Did they care about the land as much as those with deeper roots? Crombie thought about this for a moment. "First generation Canadians are special," he said. "They're neither here nor there, although they've made the basic commitment. But the second generation usually becomes completely Canadian. Look, I used to read gas meters. All over Toronto. I'd go to the back of homes. Everywhere I went, I saw little gardens, carefully tended. In apartments, window boxes. You know, Canadians have an absolute need for turf." Suddenly he laughed. "OK—to some extent I'm making myths. But there has to be some basis. You can't make myths out of nothing."

Along with the land, Canadians have a strong sense of community—to Crombie, this is another "touchstone for conservatives". At this point, I recalled Northrop Frye's assertion that Canadians have a political sense of national unity and an imaginative sense of locality, and that the tension between them is the essence of whatever the word "Canadian" means. Crombie nodded his agreement. "All you have to do is walk around this country to know that regionalism and localism are at least as strong as ever. It's not just on a larger scale—Alberta versus Ontario. It's also North York versus Toronto. Our task is not to create unity from diversity by destroying diversity. If we don't have diversity, we're in trouble. Canadians believe in tolerance and compromise and diversity—all of them conservative values. This is what Trudeau misses."

This is also where Crombie differs from Grant. "It's just not true that we're becoming a liberal, homogenized mass. This country doesn't work that way, You only have to get out and see that for yourself. It's not just a case of different regions. In any one community, there are all sorts of groups—co-ops, ethnic credit unions, and so on. They've all got different outlooks, different needs. The academics overlook those sort of things. A lot of that's missed when the theories get going."

Crombie agreed that Grant had identified real dangers, but he rejected the philosopher's ultimate pessimism. "Grant is caught in a sort of industrial determinism, and his technology is old-fashioned. In the new, post-industrial era, there will be *less* centralization, *less* standardization, more room for diversity. Computer technology leads to greater variety, more choice. It won't be a cookie cutter world."

By now Crombie was almost bursting with optimism, as he bounced along the path back to the ferry. This was catching, but I wondered how it would play among his "ordinary people". Few of them might have encountered Grant's forebodings, but millions of Canadians were struggling with the practical issues of inflation, jobs, interest rates, energy prices . . . all of these compounded by the sullen squabbles of our political masters. Surely, I suggested, it wasn't just academics who had reason to be pessimistic. Crombie acknowledged the problem, but dismissed my conclusion. "Most Canadians are optimistic by instinct. They haven't given up." To Crombie, optimism is a distinctive tory trait; in turn, this is why conservatism has strong roots among the working class. "Hope and renewal—that's what it's all about. Conservatism is edifying and uplifting. Working people instinctively want this—they understand the currency of hope. Hope is founded on the renewal of institutions, not in their replacement or destruction. Ordinary people understand the world in simple terms. If something goes wrong they're not inclined to blame the system. They recognize human limitations, and they recognize the need for hope and renewal. That's why country music is so strong in Canada. It deals with simple themes and human frailities. It offers hope."

Again I recognized my limitations: apart from anything else, I had no feeling for country music. But—I finally asked—was there any hope for the Progressive Conservatives? Crombie readily agreed that the party was hampered by its public image of being pro-big business and anti-labour, anti-ethnic, anti-women and anti-youth, as well as reactionary on most social issues. To me, this seemed a formidable burden, but Crombie was still exuding optimism. "We have to turn all that around," he said. "We have to get back to our real conservative traditions. First we show them that we're alive to social issues. Then we capitalize on the fact that the NDP is in an historic decline—we go for those votes. Then, if we could just move in the direction of Canadian nationalism, we'd be back to where Macdonald put us."

Macdonald indeed! By now I felt I'd come full circle. I had set out to explore the conservative tradition in Canada. I had started my inquiry at the turn of the century with the soaring optimism of Leacock and his fellow Imperialists—each convinced that Canada had a special destiny, based on Macdonald's vision, which was yet to be fulfilled. As we have seen, similar heady visions were proclaimed by Sandwell and Deacon even at the onset of the Great Depression. It was a hard dream to kill, especially since it rested on an innate assumption of moral and racial superiority, as well as an attachment to comfortable British ways. But it *was* anachronistic, and it was soon replaced by mediocrity and manipulation. There ensued the era of Mackenzie King and our steady absorption into the American Empire: in turn, this came to seem only one minor stage in the evolution of the whole world into the homogeneous universe of liberal technology. After the deflation of Diefenbaker, it appeared that there were no longer optimists of any stature. Lapsing into a sterile cynicism, liberals had long since squandered all their moral capital: their philosophy was bankrupt. When conservatives confronted their own traditions, they found little left to build on: as the dying Creighton lashed out with anguished fury at all those who had betrayed Macdonald's vision, the great organ voice of George Grant boomed an awesome threnody, not only for a distinctive Canada, but also for almost any concept of human diversity and individual excellence.

Along the path of this journey, however, I began to discover signs of a stubbornly residual optimism. It was there in Morton with his compassionate conservatism, and it is there in Purdy with his lyrical sense of the land, our ancestors, ourselves and our descendents — all seen as part of some larger order, some unending process. It is there in Crombie, with his visceral link to the voters, and it is there in the many younger writers and thinkers who — whatever their political leanings — have found in Creighton and Grant, not so much an excuse for despair as a bracing challenge to rectify the mistakes of their elders. To me it provided the basis for something greater than the imperative of Sir Thomas More: "When you can't make the good happen, try to prevent the very worst." Rather, it suggested that conservative values were still relevant to Canada — had never been more relevant — and that they offered a pattern for our regeneration. Even more, it seemed to me that those values *are* Canada.

On the particular level, the values are patriotic rather than anglophile, and have nothing to do with the nostalgic yearnings of our would-be country squires. Since they also have little to do with North American business liberalism, they might well cause some offence to Bay Street and the Petroleum Club, not to mention William Davis, Peter Lougheed and most of the Conservative federal caucus. As Northrop Frye has pointed out, since Canadians fought their wars of independence against the United States, it is logical that we should feel a strong suspicion of the mercantilist Whiggery which won the American Revolution (and which, in turn, evolved into the contemporary forces of liberal technology). As Frye adds: "The Canadian point of view is at once more conservative and more radical than Whiggery, closer both to aristocracy and to democracy than to oligarchy." It is Morton (and, in his own way, Purdy) who expresses this attitude most effectively to contemporary Canadians—a conservative-radical mix which is based on a sense of community and order, a feeling for the land, a respect for human diversity and human rights, a concern for social justice, and a non-ideological approach to the problems of political and economic organization. For all their vaunted pragmatism, it is liberals (and especially the Liberal party) who have consistently offended against these principles, and brought us ever closer to domination by authoritarian technocrats.

On a more philosophical level, everything starts from a sense of continuity: the Burkean view of human society as a partnership not just among the living, but among those who are living, those who are dead, and those who are yet to be born. This implies respect not only for our different roots and traditions, but also for the land itself—as our native peoples have always known, the land is something that we hold in trust. In opposition to liberal individualism, the tory sees society as an organic unity in which everyone has his duties as well as his rights. But this does not sanction bland homogeneity or an oppressive statism: although patriotic to the political concept of Canada, the tory knows that mankind finds a deeper sustenance in smaller groupings— regional, occupational, cultural or whatever. While the tory may be sophisticated, he is never merely cosmopolitan.

Because they stand for diversity, tories have an abiding concern for human rights: as Morton noted, conservatives are now the guardians of traditional liberalism. This makes them the opponents of all those modern forces which would stifle individuality and choice: big business, big unions and big government. But tories are not doctrinaire, and Canadian conservatives in particular have initiated some notable schemes of public enterprise. Their goal is never ideological purity, always social justice. At their best they are populists, treating people as individuals, rather than sociological or electoral ciphers.

Above all, it seems to me, tories have a sense of reverence. Defending human dignity, they also recognize human fallibility: man is *not* the measure of all they survey. They know that we are part of some larger order, which we can only dimly comprehend, and which must command our highest allegiance. This is the ultimate source of their optimism. If recent decades have discredited the old liberal belief in the inevitability of human progress, there is still the likelihood of some greater purpose in the universe which may yet see us through.

To me, now, it seemed hardly beyond the realm of human ingenuity that these conservative values could be translated into a political program with a strong populist clout. (It *might* be beyond the myopic abilities of the Conservative party, in which case the party would fully deserve the general disdain which it constantly courts.) Not only populist, but also radical. It would be radical to all those who call themselves tories, but proclaim the selfish shibboleths of neo-conservatism. And it would be radical to those who enact our dominant ideology: a modern liberalism which increasingly imperils the classical liberal imperatives of freedom and diversity. Building on an authentic Canadian tradition, and also responsive to the need for social justice, such a program would appeal to the optimism and pride which still reside in most Canadians.

Afterword

It's no surprise that a quarter century after its first publication, *Radical Tories: The Conservative Tradition in Canada* was selected by the *Literary Review of Canada* as one of the hundred most important Canadian books of all time. This is a beautifully written and intellectually significant work that deserves our serious attention.

Part of the continuing resonance of *Radical Tories* is surely the easy style and engaging prose of its author, journalist Charles Taylor. By writing about ideas and philosophy not as a series of antiseptic concepts, but rather as an extended conversation between close friends, Charles Taylor captures in *Radical Tories* the intellectual rigor and personal passions that shaped some of the great Canadian thinkers of the twentieth century. From Al Purdy to George Grant to Eugene Forsey to W. L. Morton, we find in *Radical Tories* a series of individual character sketches − a catalogue of verbal tics, eccentricities and intellectual foibles − which make these thinkers and their difficult and sometimes unsettling ideas accessible and alive. Charles Taylor's account, for instance, of his visits with Donald Creighton stands out as a haunting portrait of Canada's greatest historian, who, having thought long and hard about Canada's identity, is fated to live out his last days agonizing over the country's increasingly close relations with America.

However, great writing and a flare for style alone cannot save a book about politics and ideas from historical obscurity. We must look for other reasons as to why *Radical Tories* still exercises a powerful claim on our attention.

By design or unintended consequence, *Radical Tories* provides readers with an invaluable snapshot of the changing Canadian mood at an important juncture in our recent history. This was a period when the heady post-war consensus that fueled the nation-building of Lester B. Pearson, John Diefenbaker, and Pierre Trudeau had all but run out of steam. By the late 1970s, Canada was wracked by growing internal divisions and a sense of malaise about its direction. Charles Taylor's one-on-one conversations masterfully flesh out the new anxieties afflicting Canadians' sense of nationhood: our growing economic and military interdependence with America, the rise of Quebec seperatism, a loss of connection with the land and the far North, the loosening of the bonds of local community, technology's constant challenges to individual autonomy, the decline of civic participation and democratic institutions, and the growth of an impenetrable state bureaucracy. *Radical Tories* provides the reader with the philosophical context – an invaluable intellectual entry point – to the great debates of Free Trade, globalization, and national unity that consumed the country through the 1980s, 1990s, and on into the new millennium.

Beyond its friendly style and intuitive sense of the national *zeitgeist*, this book's enduring popularity ultimately rests with its passionate defence of a nationalist Tory tradition.

For Charles Taylor, this uniquely Canadian strain of conservative thought emerges first out of a steadfast commitment to the land and a responsibility for its conservation. Of equal importance are our local communities and families as the places where a person's individual life takes on context and meaning. "Radical Tories" see these types of personal connections to place and tradition as being enriched by a shared obligation to larger institutions that advance social justice and mutual care. Beyond personal values and communal structures lies the nation. Here, nationalist Tories enthusiastically espouse the virtues of nation-building and the use of the power of the state to pursue common goals which transcend region, language, and ethnicity.

The Tory nationalist creed – as seen through the writings of Stephen Leacock, Donald Creighton, and George Grant – also contains a radical program for political resistance. American preeminence, unbridled individualism, the ruthless efficiencies of the market, the large bureaucratic systems of government and business are antithetical to a Tory nationalist's vision of a just and ordered society. All are perceived as threats to sustaining the balance between individual autonomy and collective identity – at the local and national level – that provides our lives with depth and meaning. For Charles Taylor and the radical Tories, markets must be regulated, American power resisted at every turn, social and cultural institutions expanded, and the preeminence of democratic institutions defended against the courts and a rights-based political culture. In the final analysis, Canada is viewed by nationalist Tories as a unique political project that stands apart from the individualism of America and the statism of Europe; a project whose distinctness must be constantly asserted.

A quarter century on, it is difficult not to see Charles Taylor's championing of the nationalist Tory creed, and his prediction of its embrace by a nation searching for a way out of its malaise, as all but hopelessly out of date. After all, the very party that he thought could be the vehicle to promulgate a "radical" Tory agenda enthusiastically embraced free trade with America five short years after the publication of this book. Throughout the 1990s a broad political consensus emerged around a neo-liberal agenda to rein in the size of government, increase North American economic and security integration, allow for greater privatization and market de-regulation, and use the

Charter of Rights and Freedoms to assert individual and group rights.

Not only does it look as if the Tory nationalists' optimistic predictions for their political rebirth were wrong, Charles Taylor's generation's pessimism about Canada's future in the absence of a "Tory touch" seems misplaced.

The enthusiasm in the 1990s for economic globalization, new technologies and free trade did not hollow out the country's sense of itself. In fact, Canadians generally seem to have drawn newfound pride from their growing prosperity, cultural diversity, and ability to compete in global markets. More recently, with the election of the first Conservative government in over a decade, Canadians' enthusiasm for more individual choice, better relations with America, and decentralized government seems to be intensifying, with little discernible effect on the country's sense of purpose.

Did Charles Taylor fatally overreach? Is *Radical Tories* really, in the end, more of a history reference – a slice of Canadian culture circa 1983 – than a substantive treatment of the state and future of the country?

In the final analysis, this book matters not because it's a cogent analysis of conservative thought, but because it forces us to ponder the meanings and purpose of Canadian nationalism. The Radical Tory rallying cry for a uniquely Canadian identity – one that stresses the importance of place and a connection to the land, loyalty to each other and the communities we live in, concern for individual and common welfare, and the need to assert the sovereignty of the Canadian state to promote these ends – stirs what philosopher Michael Sandel called "the vague but pervasive hunger for a public life of larger meanings." Today we are all too quick to claim public celebration of a gold medal win at the Olympics or response to a patriotic beer commercial as authentic articulations of Canadian nationalism. As ephemeral expressions devoid of "larger meanings" they leave our "vague and pervasive hunger" unsatisfied, our lives somehow less than full.

Charles Taylor and the Tory nationalist tradition he espoused reminds us that we are most fulfilled when we are part of a larger whole that helps us see beyond our self-interest to support those aspects of community that underwrite the liberties and freedoms Canadians enjoy. This happens all the time in our day-to-day lives. When we are active in our communities, or immersed in family life, we are renewing the close relationships that allow us to be independent and confident in our more impersonal working and social lives.

Nations, especially democracies, follow similar rules of community and collective renewal. Countries that have healthy democratic cultures are those where individuals delay the immediate gratification of their wants and desires and assume the responsibilities of citizenship. They do so not out of blind obligation, but to be part of a larger national community that provides a texture and depth to the exercise of their individual rights and freedoms.

Twenty-five years after the publication of *Radical Tories* we would do well to reflect the humanist core of Charles Taylor's Tory nationalist philosophy.

It's not a question of enacting today a Radical Tory program of rooting out "un-Canadian" influences in our culture or stubbornly ignoring larger global trends such as free trade, technological innovation, and the opening up of Canada to influences beyond our borders. Rather, we need to be aware of the threat to our freedoms and liberties – the loss of meaningful individual autonomy in a public life without a larger purpose – posed by untrammeled pursuit of self-interest, laissez-faire economics, corporate and government bureaucracies, and, yes, blind aping of American politics and culture.

Canada is at an interesting time in its history; a juncture where questions concerning the purpose and meaning of Canadian nationalism are once again bubbling to the surface. In recent years, our confidence has been shaken in the longevity of many of the national institutions – healthcare, strong federal government, and Peacekeeping to name a few –

that have satisfied our hunger for community and belonging for the last quarter century. If modern technology, globalization, and increasing individualism continue to erode many of our most cherished institutions, then what will define us as a country? How can we remake our national institutions anew? And what are the new touchstones that could create a shared sense of national purpose?

Radical Tories performs the great service of providing Canadians with a starting point to pick up a search for answers to these basic questions. The solutions that we come up with will necessarily be different than Charles Taylor and his generation. But, as we embark on the search for a public life of larger meaning, we would do well to pause and reflect on how we can emulate the idealism and love of country of the Tory nationalist creed.

Rudyard Griffiths
Dominion Institute

Bibliography

I

Among Stephen Leacock's books, I consulted (in order of original publication):

Baldwin, Lafontaine, Hinks: Responsible Government (Toronto: Morang, 1910).

Literary Lapses (Toronto: New Canadian Library, 1957).

Sunshine Sketches of a Little Town (Toronto: New Canadian Library, 1960).

Arcadian Adventures of the Idle Rich (Toronto: New Canadian Library, 1959).

The British Empire (New York: Dodd, Mead, 1940).

Canada: The Foundations of its Future (Montreal: privately printed, 1941).

Our Heritage of Liberty (London: John Lane, 1942).

While There Is Time: The Case Against Social Catastrophe (Toronto: McClelland and Stewart, 1945).

The Boy I Left Behind Me (New York: Doubleday, 1946).

Last Leaves (Toronto: New Canadian Library, 1970).

See also:

The Social Criticism of Stephen Leacock, edited and introduced by Alan Bowker (University of Toronto Press, 1973).

The Sense of Power: Studies in the Ideas of Canadian Imperialism, 1867-1914, by Carl Berger (University of Toronto Press, 1970).

Stephen Leacock: Humourist and Humanist, by Ralph L. Curry (New York: Doubleday, 1959).

Faces of Leacock: An Appreciation, by Donald Cameron (Toronto: Ryerson, 1967).

Stephen Leacock, by Robertson Davies (Toronto: New Canadian Library, 1970).

The Man in the Panama Hat: Reminiscences of My Uncle, Stephen Leacock, by Elizabeth Kimball (Toronto: McClelland and Stewart, 1970).

Stephen Leacock: A Biography, by David M. Legate (Toronto: Macmillan of Canada, 1978).

"Stephen Leacock and the Age of Plutocracy, 1903-1921", by Ramsay Cook, in *Character and Circumstance: Essays in Honour of Donald Grant Creighton*, edited by John S. Moir (Toronto: Macmillan of Canada, 1970).

"Stephen Leacock", by Douglas Bush, in *The Canadian Imagination: Dimensions of a Literary Culture*, edited by David Staines (Harvard University Press, 1977).

Our Canada, by B. K. Sandwell (Montreal: privately printed, 1930).

My Vision of Canada, by William Arthur Deacon (Toronto: The Ontario Publishing Company, 1933).

William Arthur Deacon: A Canadian Literary Life, by Clara Thomas and John Lennox (University of Toronto Press, 1982).

II

Among Donald Creighton's works, I consulted (in order of original publication):

The Empire of the St. Lawrence (Toronto: Macmillan of Canada, 1970).

Dominion of the North (Toronto: Macmillan of Canada, 1957).

Harold Adams Innis: Portrait of a Scholar (University of Toronto Press, 1978).

The Story of Canada (Toronto: Macmillan of Canada, 1975).

John A. Macdonald: The Young Politician (Toronto: Macmillan of Canada, 1952).

John A. Macdonald: The Old Chieftain (Toronto: Macmillan of Canada) 1955).

The Road to Confederation: The Emergence of Canada, 1863-1867 (Toronto: Macmillan of Canada, 1964).

Canada's First Century (Toronto: Macmillan of Canada, 1970).

Toward the Discovery of Canada: Selected Essays (Toronto: Macmillan of Canada, 1972).

The Forked Road: Canada 1939-1957 (Toronto: Macmillan of Canada, 1976).

Takeover: A Novel (Toronto: McClelland and Stewart, 1978).

The Passionate Observer: Selected Writings, edited by Ramsay Derry (Toronto: McClelland and Stewart, 1980).

"Canada in the English-Speaking World", *The Canadian Historical Review*, Vol. XXVI, 1945.

See also:

The Writing of Canadian History, by Carl Berger (Toronto: Oxford, 1976), Chapter Nine.

Character and Circumstance: Essays in Honour of Donald Grant Creighton, edited by John S. Moir (Toronto: Macmillan of Canada, 1970). See the Publisher's Foreward by John Gray; "Donald Grant Creighton" by John S. Moir, and "Donald Creighton and Canadian History" by J. M. S. Careless.

Freedom Wears a Crown, by John Farthing, edited by Judith Robinson (Toronto: Kingswood House, 1957).

III

Among W. L. Morton's works, I consulted:

The Kingdom of Canada (Toronto: McClelland and Stewart, 1963).
The Critical Years: The Union of British North America, 1857-1873 (Toronto: McClelland and Stewart, 1964).
Manitoba: A History (University of Toronto Press, 1967).
The Canadian Identity, Second Edition (University of Toronto Press, 1972).
Contents of Canada's Past: Selected Essays of W. L. Morton, edited and with an introduction by A. B. McKillop (Toronto: Carleton Library, 1980).

See also:

The Writing of Canadian History, by Carl Berger (Toronto: Oxford, 1976), Chapter Ten.
The Maple Leaf Forever: Essays on Nationalism and Politics in Canada, by Ramsay Cook (Toronto: Macmillan of Canada, 1971), pp 158-162.
My Country, Canada or Quebec, by Solange Chaput Rolland (Toronto: Macmillan of Canada, 1966). Introduction by W. L. Morton.
"Canadian History" by Michael S. Cross, in *Literary History of Canada*, Second Edition, Volume Three, general editor Carl F. Klinck (University of Toronto Press, 1976), pp. 65-67.
The Conservative Mind, by Russell Kirk, sixth revised edition (South Bend: Gateway Editions, 1978).
Reflections on the Revolution in France, by Edmund Burke, edited by Conor Cruise O'Brien (London: Penguin, 1979).

IV

Among Al Purdy's books, I consulted:

North of Summer: Poems from Baffin Island (Toronto: McClelland and Stewart, 1967).

Selected Poems (Toronto: McClelland and Stewart, 1972).

Sex and Death (Toronto: McClelland and Stewart, 1973).

In Search for Owen Roblin (Toronto: McClelland and Stewart, 1974).

Sundance at Dusk (Toronto: McClelland and Stewart, 1976).

No Other Country (Toronto: McClelland and Stewart, 1977).

Being Alive (Toronto: McClelland and Stewart, 1978).

The Stone Bird (Toronto: McClelland and Stewart, 1981).

See also:

The New Romans: Candid Opinions of the U.S., edited by Al Purdy (Edmonton: Hurtig, 1968).

Al Purdy, by George Bowering (Toronto: Copp Clark, 1970).

For Openers: Conversations with 24 Canadian Writers, by Alan Twigg, (Madiera Park, B.C.: Harbour Publishing, 1981), pp. 1-11.

Canadian Literature: Surrender or Revolution, by Robin Mathews (Toronto: Steel Rail, 1978).

Gardens, Covenants, Exiles: Loyalism in the Literature of Upper Canada/Ontario, by Dennis Duffy (University of Toronto Press, 1982), Chapter Seven.

V

Freedom and Order: Collected Essays, by Eugene Forsey (Toronto: McClelland and Stewart, 1974).

The Politics of John W. Dafoe and the Free Press, by Ramsey Cook (University of Toronto Press, 1963).

The League for Social Reconstruction: Intellectual Origins of the Democratic Left in Canada, 1930-1942, by Michiel Horn (University of Toronto Press, 1980).

A Nation Unaware: The Canadian Economic Culture, by Herschel Hardin (Vancouver: J. J. Douglas, 1974).

Canadian Labour in Politics, by Gad Horowitz (University of Toronto Press, 1968). Chapter One.

VI

In order of original publication, George Grant's books are:

The Empire, Yes or No? (Toronto: Ryerson, 1945).

Philosophy in the Mass Age (Toronto: Copp Clark, 1966).

Lament for a Nation: The Defeat of Canadian Nationalism (Toronto: McClelland and Stewart, 1965).

Technology and Empire: Perspectives on North America (Toronto: Anansi, 1969).

English-Speaking Justice (Sackville: Mount Allison University, 1978).

See also:

George Grant in Process: Essays and Conversations, edited by Larry Schmidt (Toronto: Anansi, 1978).

Principal Grant, by William Lawson Grant and Frederick Hamilton (Toronto: Morang, 1904).

Ocean to Ocean, by George Munro Grant (Toronto: Coles Reprints, 1979).

The Sense of Power: Studies in the Ideas of Canadian Imperialism, 1867-1914, by Carl Berger (University of Toronto Press, 1970).

The Maple Leaf Forever; Essays on Nationalism and Politics in Canada, by Ramsay Cook (Toronto: Macmillan of Canada, 1971), Chapter Four.

"Have We a Canadian Nation?" by George Grant, *Public Affairs*, Vol. VIII, 1945.

"An Ethic of Community" by George Grant, in *Social Purpose for Canada*, edited by Michael Oliver (University of Toronto Press, 1961).

"Tories, Socialists and the Demise of Canada" by Gad Horowitz, *Canadian Dimension*, May-June, 1965.

"From Roosevelt to L.B.J." by George Grant, in *The New Romans: Candid Opinions of the U.S.*, edited by Al Purdy (Edmonton: Hurtig, 1968).

"A Conversation on Technology and Man", Gad Horowitz and George Grant, *Journal of Canadian Studies*, Vol. 4, August, 1969.

"George Grant: Language, Nation, The Silence of God" by Eli Mandel, *Canadian Literature*, No. 83, Winter, 1979.

VII

Canada and the Canadian Question, by Goldwin Smith (University of Toronto Press, 1971).

Goldwin Smith: Victorian Liberal, by Elisabeth Wallace (University of Toronto Press, 1957).

"Goldwin's Myth" by Wayne Roberts, *Canadian Literature*, No. 83, Winter 1979.

In Search of Canadian Liberalism, by Frank H. Underhill (Toronto: Macmillan of Canada, 1960).

The Writing of Canadian History, by Carl Berger (Toronto: Oxford, 1976), pp. 54-84; 195-201.

"The Writing of Canadian History" by William Kilbourn, in *Contexts of Canadian Criticism*, edited by Eli Mandel (University of Toronto Press, 1971).

"The Ogdensburg Agreement and F. H. Underhill" by Donald Creighton, in *The Passionate Observer: Selected Writings*, edited by Ramsay Derry (Toronto: McClelland and Stewart, 1980).

The Affluent Society, by John Kenneth Galbraith (Boston: Houghton Mifflin, 1958).

The Scotch, by John Kenneth Galbraith (Toronto: Macmillan of Canada, 1964).

The New Industrial State, by John Kenneth Galbraith (Boston: Houghton Mifflin, 1967).

A Life in Our Times, by John Kenneth Galbraith (Boston: Houghton Mifflin, 1981).

The Literary Politicians, by Mitchell S. Ross (New York: Doubleday, 1978), pp. 111-162.

Federalism and the French Canadians, by Pierre Elliott Trudeau (Toronto: Macmillan of Canada, 1968).

Shrug: Trudeau in Power, by Walter Stewart (Toronto: New Press, 1971).

Paradox: Trudeau as Prime Minister, by Anthony Westell (Scarborough: Prentice-Hall, 1972).

Trudeau, by George Radwanski (Toronto: Macmillan of Canada, 1978).

The Northern Magus: Pierre Trudeau and Canadians, by Richard Gwyn (Toronto: McClelland and Stewart, 1980).

The Liberal Idea of Canada, by James Laxer and Robert Laxer (Toronto: Lorimer, 1977).

Political Parties and Ideologies in Canada, by W. Christian and C. Campbell (Toronto: McGraw Hill Ryerson, 1974).

VIII

Stanfield, by Geoffrey Stevens (Toronto: McClelland and Stewart, 1973).

Discipline of Power: The Conservative Interlude and the Liberal Restoration, by Jeffrey Simpson (Toronto: Personal Library, 1980).

The Tiny Perfect Mayor: David Crombie and Toronto's Reform Aldermen, by Jon Caufield (Toronto: Lorimer, 1974).

The Bush Garden: Essays on the Canadian Imagination, by Northrop Frye (Toronto: Anansi, 1971).

Index